FLYING TO NORWAY,
GROUNDED IN BURMA

Previous publications by the same author:

Norwegian Patrol, Airlife 1985
Head in the Clouds, Airlife 1996

About fifty magazine articles: *c.*30 in *Aeroplane Monthly* and *Flypast*, others in *The Oldie, Money & Family Wealth, Cheshire Life, Trout & Salmon*

FLYING TO NORWAY, GROUNDED IN BURMA

BY

Goronwy Edwards DFC, MA, BDS

Pen & Sword
AVIATION

First published in
Great Britain in 2008
By Pen and Sword Aviation
An imprint of
Pen and Sword Books Ltd
47 Church Street
Barnsley
South Yorkshire
S70 2AS

Copyright © Goronwy Edwards 2008

ISBN 978 1 84415 8096

Printed and bound by Biddles, Kings Lynn

Pen and Sword Books Ltd incorporates the imprints of Pen and
Sword Aviation, Pen and Sword Maritime, Pen and Sword Military,
Wharncliffe Local History, Pen and Sword Select, Pen and Sword
Military Classics and Leo Cooper.

For a complete list of Pen and Sword titles please contact
Pen and Sword Books Limited
47 Church Street, Barnsley, South Yorkshire, S70 2AS, England
E-mail: enquiries@pen-and-sword.co.uk
Website: www.pen-and-sword.co.uk

Contents

Dedication

This book is dedicated to all those who have suffered from Post-Traumatic Stress Disorder, in whatever subtle or unsubtle way it manifests itself, in both military and civilian life. And also to those who had to put up with them during their lows – in my case Christine, my well-beloved wife of many years.

Acknowledgements

To Derek Grossmark, Barrie Johnson and Ela Dwornikowska, for their invaluable technical assistance to a computer illiterate during my pre-publication problems.

Chapter One

The Fledgling

With the end of The Great War in 1918, many ex-Flying Corps pilots made a living of sorts by travelling the country, flying out of farmers' fields and offering joyrides at five shillings (25p) a time. Known as 'barnstormers', they lived simply and frugally, their outfits consisting of a mechanic, a bell tent in which they both slept, and a truck serving as a travelling workshop. Their aircraft were usually war-surplus Avro biplanes with rotary engines, in which the radial cylinders whirled round a fixed crankshaft. They advertised in the local papers, flew low over the towns and nailed their posters to telegraph poles, and it was one such poster that my two brothers had seen. They'd rushed home and persuaded my father to blue a pound on a flight for the four of us.

When that old Avro rumbled across Dick Vaughan's field in South Wales in 1926 and bounced gently into the air I knew that flying would have to be the life for me.

And flying was much in the news. Imperial Airways, working out of Croydon, was already sending its four-engined Handley Pages to Egypt in two days, with talk of extending to India and South Africa. In 1928 Bert Hinkler flew from England to Australia in fifteen days, a third of the time taken by the P & O liners to sail the distance. And three years after that Amy Johnson cut Hinkler's time to nine days!

The world was shrinking fast.

But getting into aviation was the problem. In no way could my mother, widowed at 38 and with four children, afford to train me as a pilot, which cost about £1,000, they said. Some day, somehow, I would get into the air again, but in the meantime I had to make do with flying my model aircraft. Its fuselage was a single stick of spruce, its wings a silk-covered open framework and its motive power twisted strands of rubber. By winding the propeller backwards through the recommended hundred turns, plus a dozen or so extra that the instruction manual warned would over-stress the model, it flew for about twenty seconds. Flying this model in Bob Probert's field one day I became aware that a faint droning that had been part of the background for some time had grown rapidly in volume, and a Hart light-bomber of the Royal Air Force appeared over the hill and slid down into the valley. The roar of its 500 hp engine died away as the pilot cut the throttle and glided towards the field, as though to land. The big biplane, with the wind sighing gently in its bracing wires, came low over the hedge, and I waited for this heaven-sent opportunity to see a powerful military aircraft close up, and for the chance to talk to its demi-god of a pilot. But he aborted the landing, went round again to made another attempt, then yet a third, before deciding that the field was too small for his forced landing. He flew away over the hill.

But he'd made me realise that the time of day-dreaming was past: that I had to do something to get a foothold in aviation. My eldest brother, by sheer hard work, they said, had won a scholarship to university. Maybe I could do the same, and as Cambridge was the only university offering a degree in aeronautical engineering it looked as though Cambridge it was going to be.

To the astonishment of my teachers, I started to work at school, and to get rid of the previous term's despairing 'Yet he has the ability' type of report. I matriculated, but the only positive result was that my mother's brother, Uncle Dick – the titular male head of the family since my father's death – offered to get me a job as an articled clerk to a chartered accountant. Mr Roberts wore bat-winged collars with his pin-striped suit, the only type of suit he was ever seen in, come sunshine, hail, snow or sleet. He was worthy, dull, and enthusiastic about figures, though only of the non-female kind. A lifetime in his office would be akin to the knell of doom, but it was, of course, a job, and not to be sniffed at in the Hungry Thirties.

And then the advertisement appeared in one of my flying magazines: 'Applications will be considered for Short Service Commissions in the General Duties (Flying) Branch of the Royal Air Force.' The educational requirements were well within my grasp, and my age would soon be right, not less than 17¾ There was no difficulty in winning over my mother, but the big one would be Uncle Dick. I approached the presence.

'Fly!' he snorted, 'You mean fly for a *living*! You must be mad. Just think of Willie Bailey.'

Silently, I cursed the late Willie Bailey. A First World War survivor, and a rich guy, he had bought a war-surplus Avro, but had looped the loop once too often and killed himself.

Not a good start, but I had one card left, because from the moment of shaking the dust of North Wales from my feet I would be self-supporting, which would help the tottering finances of the family no end. This self-sufficiency appealed to me immensely, as I was fed up with having to wear my older brothers' cast-off clothes, especially the shoes, which had now replaced boots as the accepted form of footwear. There was little problem in wearing an over-size pair of boots as the laces round your ankles held them securely in place, but oversize shoes were another kettle of fish altogether. To my embarrassment, occasionally one would fall off, despite the curling down of my toes in an attempt to keep them on.

I returned to the fray, and played a timorous ace. Uncle Dick was known locally as 'Mad Dick', having earned the title as a graduate of the Toad School of Motoring. He was addicted to powerful American cars, which he drove flat out for most of the time, scattering the Welsh peasantry like chaff before him. He regarded pedestrians as belonging to those two religious categories the quick and the dead, and when Mad Dick was around people took the hint and ran for cover. When Uncle Dick opined that anyone who wanted to fly for a living must be mad, the 1936 equivalent of the crunch had come. If I didn't beat him on this, I'd be a penguin to the end of my days. I looked my fellow madman firmly in the eye.

'There are some in the village who think it would be a darned sight safer in the cockpit of an aeroplane than riding round as a passenger in that Studebaker of yours', I retorted, appalled at my rashness, but bitterly disappointed at the high-pitched squeak in which the protest had been delivered.

Uncle Dick inhaled deeply and went purple. But as my knees shook the purple diminished to red, then merely to bright pink. He put his pipe back in his mouth, grunted like a wounded boar, and played his ace.

'It's a Short Service Commission. What will you do after four years, when you're flung out on to the Reserve for six years. You'll have no job. There are still an awful lot of unemployed, you know.'

'I'll have my gratuity of £300, all the money I will have saved during my four years' service' – that would have been good for a laugh had either of us known it – 'and there are correspondence courses I can study in the meantime. When I come out in September 1940 I'll be just in time to go to Cambridge and start an aeronautical engineering course.'

Impressed by my planning, he grunted, 'All right, you might as well apply, I suppose. But there's this civil war in Spain, you know, and it looks as though Hitler's spoiling for a European war. He's got his eye on Austria and Czechoslovakia, and his *Luftwaffe*'s streets ahead of the Royal Air Force in numbers, you know.'

'That's why the RAF is expanding and needs pilots. We mean to stop him.'

Uncle Dick was a kindly man, and forbore to cast any doubts on the value of my contribution to this blocking move, so the day before I achieved that age of 17¾. I sent in my application to the Air Ministry. My interview and medical being successful, in 1936 I travelled to Sywell, near Northampton, where Brooklands Aviation had a flying school for the initial training of RAF pilots on the simple Tiger Moth. We were still civilians, so if we showed no aptitude for flying we could be returned to civilian life without all the rigmarole that dismissal from a fighting service would have entailed.

Despite dressing like Teddy bears in our layers of flying clothing, nothing could keep out the cold of that freezing winter of 1936. If I was flying solo I would beat my hands on my knees to get some sort of circulation going, and as the pain grew worse I shouted all the obscenities I knew into the slipstream. If I was flying under dual instruction, however, the blasphemies had to be silent, so weren't half as effective.

I had also been 'fitted' with a helmet that was a size too large, so that the slipstream roared and whistled between my cheeks and the loosely fitting thing, and made the words of wisdom coming down the voice tube from the front cockpit difficult to understand. Whereas *I* thought my instructor was doing his party-piece imitation of Donald Duck, *he* thought he had a halfwit on his hands, and relations were a bit strained when we landed from our first trip.

This helmet was my first introduction to the more tortuous side of service life, the 'usual channels' and so on. When I asked for a replacement the storekeeper explained that, as a civilian, he could do little about second-hand Air Force property. I came back with the fact that he had measured me for the darned thing, so it was *his* job to ensure a perfect fit, upon which he launched into a dissertation of what exactly would be needed to reverse the decision. Apparently it was going to take the personal intervention of the Chief of the Air Staff, Marshal of the Royal Air Force Lord Trenchard KG, DSO, DFC, etc. 'My hands are tied', he cried, a highly inaccurate statement, as he was waving them in the air as he spoke. I gave up, and bought myself a well-fitting helmet from the flying club across the field.

I was chuffed to go solo before my 18th birthday, but first had to learn the recovery from the spin, and I concluded that only the mentally deranged could possibly like their first one. As the speed dies away the aircraft starts to wallow, then to shudder, and *then* comes the God-awful bit – the nose drops like a plummet, your stomach rises into your throat, and a gigantic hand grips one wingtip and whirls the aircraft round in mad gyrations as you dive vertically earthwards. It isn't done to scream in terror, of course, but eventually the machine obeys your input to the controls and regains normal flight. Eventually, in fact, I got to *like* spins.

Towards the end of the course the constitutional crisis leading to the abdication of King Edward VIII surfaced, coming as a complete surprise to the country, as hitherto the Establishment had had great control over the media, and had suppressed all news of the King's liaison with Mrs Simpson. As the drama approached its climax the universal feeling was the unthinkability of a twice-divorced American socialite becoming even the morganatic consort of the King. Popular as he was, this was one thing he couldn't have, and behind the sadness and sympathy for him was the disappointment that he could contemplate ditching the heritage of the British Empire to become, who knew, perhaps the third divorced husband of Wallis Simpson. And so the shy and retiring Duke of York was forced into the job, but obviously had great support from his vivacious wife, the former Lady Elizabeth Bowes-Lyon.

We survivors of the Sywell course went on to the RAF Depot at Uxbridge for a fortnight's disciplinary and drill training, during which we were commissioned as acting pilot officers on probation – and under suspicion half the time, we felt. We gathered from our drill sergeants that there were few lower forms of animal life in the service, and they voiced humiliating public assessments of our ability at square-bashing without being in any way insubordinate by simply added the suffix 'Sir' to each stream of insults. Chastening though it was when you were the target, I must say that it was thoroughly enjoyable when somebody else was copping it.

We now drew our uniform allowance of £50, and I was relieved to find that Gieves, my approved military tailor, could kit me out for £49 19s 6d, which would leave enough over for a pint or so of bitter. But the lists omitted to mention that only one of each item was included in the offer, and you can't get very far socially with only one shirt and one pair of socks to your name, so we all had to spend at least £60. But this was no problem, as in the genteelest possible way we were introduced to the hire-purchase system, then in its infancy.

'If you would like to sign this form, sir, for one pound a month – or more should you wish – we will forward it to your bankers – Cox and Kings in St James's I presume, sir? Yes, I'm sure it is', he continued, implying that anyone not banking there was beneath consideration. As five shillings (25p) a week was all that the kitty would stand, I signed a pound-a-month banker's order to Gieves, and started an association with them that lasted for years. Their shop in Bond Street, before it was destroyed by the *Luftwaffe* in 1941, was a militarian's delight. In glass cases were miniature figures a foot in height in the uniforms of all branches of the services, and the moment you entered you felt a part of British history. The forebears of the men represented by those midget figures had fought in all the wars from Cromwell onwards, and in such an atmosphere you usually ended up buying more kit than you needed, the bills mounting proportionately. In fact when, some four years later, Winston Churchill pronounced his immortal words about the Battle of Britain that 'Never in the field of human conflict was so much owed by so many to so few', those of us not entirely clued up thought that he was referring to the amounts we all owed our military tailors.

Among the publications issued to us was the RAF Pocket Book, straight out of a modern *Outward Bound* course, but twenty times better, being in the style of Rudyard Kipling and Fennimore Cooper. It gave advice on every possible contingency which could face us upholders of the British Empire. It refreshed us on zogging – the semaphore-type arm-signalling used in open-cockpit aircraft before we had wireless communication – a bit like the tick-tack men on racecourses. Should you fly over a Royal Navy ship flying flags with crisses and crosses, stars and bars, and stripes in all directions, Page 34 would tell you whether the ship was about to sink with all hands or whether the captain was having a blitz on his crew's personal hygiene. You had been shot down by Waziri tribesmen firing muzzle-loading *jezails* that they'd loaded a couple of Ramadans ago, and wished to retain your ability to father children? Pages 84/5 gave examples of the ghoolie chits you would be issued with if serving on the North-West Frontier. These, printed in all the languages of that complex country, promised money if the hostage was returned intact.

I also think it told you how to cook a lizard, just in case you were unfortunate enough to have had an engine die on you while over lizard country.

Though I was commissioned when Edward VIII was on the throne, it took some time for my written commission to be handed to me. A confirmed traditionalist, even at the age of 18, I revelled in its archaic seventeenth-century style: its use of capital letters and punctuation. But regretted that it wasn't given under the hand of Edward VIII, which would have made it a relatively rare document:

> George VI by the Grace of God, OF GREAT BRITAIN, IRELAND AND THE BRITISH DOMINIONS BEYOND THE SEA, KING, DEFENDER OF THE FAITH, EMPEROR OF INDIA, &C.
>
> To our trusty and well beloved Goronwy Edwards Greeting:
>
> We reposing especial Trust and Confidence in your Loyalty, Courage, and good conduct, do by these Presents Constitute and Appoint you to be an Officer in Our Royal Air Force from the Twenty-first day of December 1936. You are therefore carefully and diligently to discharge your Duty as such in the rank of Acting Pilot Officer or in such higher Rank as We may from time to time hereafter be pleased to promote or appoint you to, of which a notification will be made in the London Gazette, and you are at all times to exercise and well discipline in their Duties both the inferior Officers and Airmen serving under you and use your best endeavours to keep them in good Order and Discipline. And we do hereby Command them to Obey you as their superior Officer and you to observe and follow such Orders and Directions as from time to time you may receive from Us, or any your superior Officer, according to the Rules and Discipline of War, in pursuance of the Trust hereby reposed in you.
>
> Given at Our Court, at St. James's the Seventeenth day of August 1937 in the First Year of Our Reign.
>
> By His Majesty's Command.

It was signed by Lord Stansgate, then Minister for Air. He was Tony Benn's father, and whether it was this sort of flannel that caused Tony to cast off his titles and other sorts of bull I've never bothered to find out, as at that time I was all for it.

The Uxbridge disciplinary course came to an end, and we all dispersed for Christmas leave before going on to our Service Flying Training Schools, in my case to No. 10 FTS at Tern Hill in Shropshire, where we flew the fabulous Hart that I'd first seen that day back in Probert's field. With a top speed of 184 mph, the Hart, when introduced in 1930, had mucked up the next year's air defences by being ten miles an hour faster than the current fighter, the Bulldog, which just couldn't catch it.

In the Junior Term we repeated all that we had learned on our little Tiger Moths, but on these charismatic 500 hp machines. And we now did additional exercises such as forced-landing practice in case the engine conked, this being practised on a variety of farmers' fields rented for the purpose. The instructor would close the throttle on you and say, 'Okay, your engine's cut. Set her down in the best field you can find.'

We approached, as though to land, and if the grazing animals scattered that's what the farmer was paid for. As you came low over the hedge your instructor would assess just how well you had made it, when you opened up and flew away. Many of the animals became so blasé about the whole business that even 500 snarling horsepower streaking twenty feet above would not persuade them to lift their heads from the serious business of grazing. If one had had to do a genuine forced landing in such a field there could have been a fair amount of scrap metal and beef steaks strewn about the place.

On one particular day Flying Officer Hamilton, my instructor, closed the throttle, told me to get on with it, and approved the field I'd selected.

'Now Edwards, I want you to land it. Set her down well into the field, as it's better to hit the far hedge slowly than the near one fast. Treat this as the real thing. *Land* it.'

What fun! I side-slipped off excess height, straightened out, landed, and we rumbled to a stop.

'Taxi back downwind, keep the brakes on and open the throttle a bit; we don't want the engine to stall.'

I was surprised to see Hamilton throw off his straps, get out of the aircraft and stand in the steps alongside my cockpit.

'Have you got a handkerchief?'

'Yes, thank you all the same, sir.'

'A clean one?'

Well, he'd never find out, would he?

'I'd like to borrow it.'

Odd, but I handed over what turned out to be a clean one, eminently suitable for the august nose of my instructor. He climbed down, walked away and stooped, sweeping his hands from side to side before rising to his full height, repeating the process from time to time. Strange, I thought. Maybe he's a member of some obscure religious sect – he came from a long line of military men. Maybe his grandfather had converted to Islam when in India, or something.

He carried on with downcast eyes, the noise of the engine preventing me from hearing the incantations which he was undoubtedly uttering. But time was passing, and despite the fact that the radiator was wound fully out, the engine temperature was rising, and I wondered how long I was going to be stuck in an undersized field with a superior officer of suspect mental stability.

However, it looked as though the gods had finally been propitiated, as Hamilton, with a bulging handkerchief in each hand, came back and hooked his elbows over the side of the cockpit.

'Edwards,' he said, 'I want a smooth, gentle take-off and an equally good landing. I don't want any of these mushrooms broken.'

'*Mushrooms*, sir?'

'Mushrooms. D'you think I'd leave a valuable aircraft in charge of an acting pilot officer – er, still on probation, aren't you? Thought as much – unless I had a very good reason. Best mushroom field in Shropshire, this. Now don't forget that pansy landing back at Tern Hill. Also don't forget that we have to log the whole trip as flying time, so don't deduct our time on the ground. Put down something that takes twenty minutes or so, like 'Use of the mixture control at medium altitudes.' That'll account for the extra. Not that people mind too much as long as you're not *seen* doing it. And while we are on the subject of extra-curricular activities Edwards, I don't mind, within reason, what you get up to in the air as long as you bear two things in mind. One you will already have worked out – don't be *seen* doing it.'

'And the other, sir?'

'Whatever you get up to in the air, don't hit the ground while doing it.'

I felt that the RAF lifestyle was going to suit me.

An aesthetic pleasure when doing aerobatics in the Hart was provided by its gravity-feed petrol tank up in the top wing. An air vent opened from this, and when you were inverted, as in a slow roll, a steady stream of petrol flowed out, immediately vaporising into a snow-white plume streaming away below your head. It was a very pretty sight, and if you held the aircraft on its back for some time you could get rid of quite a bit of taxpayers' money as you indulged your artistic tastes, the limiting factor being the length of time you could stand being inverted before your eyeballs popped out.

The current advertisement for Reckitt's Blue, which washed clothes as white as any whitener plugged on TV nowadays, was an azure sea in which an attractive girl drove a speedboat, its wake a dazzling white. 'Out of the Blue comes the Whitest Wash', proclaimed the hoardings. I could get the same result on a cloudless day by turning the Hart upside down and shoving the nose further above the horizon than was really needed, so that the white spray was seen against the blueness of the sky. I would have liked to sell my idea to Reckitt's publicity men, but felt that 'any superior officer', as my commission had it, might get too inquisitive as to the source of my inspiration and clamp down on my pleasure.

Inevitably, one has off-days. I'd made a mess of an aerobatic half hour, and back on the ground Hamilton was going through it all again.

'Edwards, you fly an aeroplane with a degree of delicacy; like a violinist playing the fiddle: you don't beat it like a bass drum. Sawdust doesn't fly, you know.'

'Sawdust, sir?'

'It's a hangover from the days when aircraft were made of wood. If you mishandled a wooden aircraft to the extent that it broke up on you, that's about all you'd be left with – a couple of bags of sawdust.'

I filed the advice for future reference.

We now started night-flying, ground instruction on the flare-path being the first step, and I found it a very romantic business. In those pre-concrete-runway days a flare-path of goose-neck paraffin flares was laid in the form of a T, avoiding soft spots in the ground due to recent rain, newly laid grass, etc. The flares produced a red, smoky flame that would burn for hours. The level of illumination was negligible, the flames being used purely as a landing mark, and the smoke a check on possible changes in the wind direction. The floodlight – a massive searchlight affair – was tested, and from then on its generator ran all night, the noise of its diesel muting when the light was switched off, but rising to a full-throated roar when it came on again.

Once darkness fell all aircraft movements had to be interpreted by the relative positions of the red light on the port wingtip, the green on the starboard and the white on the tail, and we controlled them with red, green and white Aldis lamps; with a Very pistol as backup in case of failure. These had enormous 1½-inch calibre barrels, and fired their coloured signal flares with a pronounced recoil and a hell of a bang.

The roar of the floodlight generator drowned out all other sounds, so the aircraft's lights flitted silently above us like fireflies, altering position as they turned this way and that on their circuits. When they lined up on the flare-path, their ticking-over propellers were diaphanous circles in the reflected glow of the goose-necks. When given the green to take off they whirled into invisibility as the throttle opened, flames streamed from their exhausts, and the machine would vanish into the darkness, the white tail-light twitching from side to side as the pilot made rudder corrections.

The landings were equally fascinating. The silently approaching red and green wingtip lights grew wider and wider apart, and sank lower and lower as the aircraft neared its goal. Then the floodlight would be switched on, and into the light-soaked area the Hart would fly, its propeller reflecting a shimmering image of the floodlight's beam, before slowing into that diaphanous disc again as the pilot cut the throttle and sank to earth.

At intervals we would be sent on lonely expeditions to check on the flares, a half-hour release into a world of your own. Now away from the roar of the generator, you could hear your term-mates' engines again, and you walked from one smoking flare to another, checking its paraffin reservoir, but keeping an eye open in case an aircraft swung on landing or take-off and one of your pals made a dirty dart at you.

Eventually the time came for my own night-flying instruction. With Hamilton's advice coming down the earphones I sped down the flare-path, where the occasional ghostly figure standing by one of the flares flitted past, and with a few final rumbles and bounces the Hart was airborne. Above the invisible trees the horizon appeared – that faint indication of where the sky ended and the earth began – and I climbed away to join the circuit. When my green-to-land came up I turned in on finals, gauging the approach by the apparent closeness-together of the flares – too close together and you were too low, too far apart too high. At the last moment the floodlight came on, I flew like a Moth into its brilliant white light, and landed. One more step up the ladder!

A variation in night landings was that using wingtip flares. These were magnesium candles a foot long, held in brackets under the lower wing. Fired electrically from the cockpit, they gave an intense white light which did not blind the pilot as they were blanketed by the wing. But a disadvantage was that, once fired, there was no further control over it: it had to burn itself out, and on the ground the tremendous heat could damage the linen fabric of the wing. If it was still burning after the landing one taxied fast to keep up a good flow of cooling air, pursued by a cursing band of fire-fighters lugging their heavy extinguishers.

Later on we used the Audax for night-flying, its twelve-foot exhaust pipes becoming things of beauty at night. The first half glowed a bright cherry-red, which gave me a fright the first time I looked outboard, and this was followed by six feet of pipe perforated with dozens of holes to allow the gases to escape sideways. The slipstream had cooled them by the time they arrived in this section so that its length was filled with an ethereal, flickering blue light, visible through all the holes. I used to stick my head over the side of the cockpit and, with the cold night air battering away at my face, watch that flickering light and feel worlds away from those unfortunate millions out there in the darkness, confined to the surface of the earth.

Inevitably, after a while, I had to abandon my dream world and return to another pleasure – that of guiding this throbbing flying machine through the black velvet night skies.

I got a fright while practising a solo forced landing. I'd wound the radiator in to keep the engine warm on the glide, had made a fairly good pass at the field and climbed away at full throttle. At 1,500 feet a plume of smoke emerged from under the engine cowling; not just a wisp, but a solid, evil tube of smoke streaming back along the right-hand side of the cockpit.

FIRE! About the most frightening experience that can happen in the air. 'Action in the event of fire in the air' had been rammed into my head, and there was a good incentive to learn it as the main petrol tank of the Hart, holding 85 gallons, was just the other side of the instrument panel, less than a foot from one's knees – 'Turn off the petrol, open the throttle fully to get rid of all the fuel in the pipes, close the throttle, push the fire-extinguisher button', they'd told us.

'Fire! Hell, I'm on fire!'

Alas, my training went out of the window as fast as I started to go over the side. Forgetting everything, I ripped off my safety harness, reached for the grab-handles in the top wing, and put one foot on the exhaust pipe, preparing to dive steeply downwards to avoid being struck by the tailplane, which could do anything from cracking a few ribs to breaking your neck in the powerful slipstream.

'Don't forget to count three before you open your parachute', said my guardian angel.

'Thanks, mate', I acknowledged. Then took a last look at the smoke before leaving for ever. 'Come to think of it, it's *white* smoke, not grey', raced my brain. 'More like steam than smoke. Steam! My God! I've boiled the engine!'

I'd forgotten to wind the radiator out after my forced-landing practice, and the full-throttle climb, with inadequate air flowing through the radiator, had done the trick. 'As pants the Hart for cooling streams when heated in the chase', as *Hymns Ancient & Modern* had it. (And possibly future editions of the *Pilots' Handling Notes for the Hart and Audax Aircraft.*)

Thoroughly ashamed of myself, I clawed my way back into the cockpit against the battering of the slipstream, wound out the radiator, re-strapped myself in, and slunk back to Tern Hill, going through the fire drill again, and thankful that there'd been no one around to witness the scene.

Behind one of the hangars was a graveyard of elderly cars abandoned by our predecessors as being beyond reasonable repair, and they were there for the asking. To teenagers of the economic underclass things like road tax and log-books were figments of the imagination, and I saved a further five shillings as I hadn't yet got around to buying a driving licence. Gibson, another schoolboy entrant, and I did a tour of the graveyard when we considered that we were financially stable enough to run an untaxed and uninsured car, our eventual choice being an open Alvis 12/50 racer which had already lost its hood, but had the advantage that its ancient tax disc was almost the same colour as that of the current year. It lacked any form of self-starting system, even a winding-handle, so that it had to be push-started. It had a lighting system, but lacked a battery, so we always had to get home before dark, or formate on co-operative team mates, preferably two, with us in the middle. We rarely exceeded sixty miles an hour in it, as the slightly insecure bonnet used to fly off above this speed. We were nearly decapitated the first time it happened, as however strong the string we used to tie it down it wore through eventually. As soon as the lid started the wild hammering which foretold its imminent flight, we ducked beneath the windscreen until the final screech of metal, followed by a darkening of the sky, gave us the information that we could now raise our heads in safety again, stop, and recover the equipment.

We sped up along the Shropshire lanes, extending our knowledge of the Shrewsbury bars, and were all set for the happiest of impecunious summers until, as we swept over a hump-back bridge, a puppy ran out and vanished beneath the car. I stopped, feeling very sorry for the puppy, then even sorrier for myself, as the village bobby was leaning against a wall twenty yards away. With my hideously illegal car I visualised the court action that lay ahead, followed, no doubt, by a request that I resign my commission as being a disgrace to the service. I wondered, in my misery, if Mr Roberts was still holding open that ghastly vacancy in his chartered accountant's office.

By contrast the village bobby seemed very comfortable, and a scuffle beneath the car led to the reappearance of the puppy, apparently none the worse for wear. The constable took his pipe out of his mouth, said, 'Dog's all right, zur', and replaced the pipe. As far as he was concerned the incident was closed. But we were stuck with a stalled engine and a tax disc as off colour as I was. I hissed to Gibson to get out of the car and stand in front of the tax disc, and asked the policeman if he'd kindly lend a hand to push-start us. He took a cliff-hanging twenty seconds to remove his pipe and knock out the ash before giving the car such a shove that it started immediately, the unprepared Gibson having to grab the back of the hood and scrabble his way over the petrol tank and into the back seat before he could rejoin me in the front. We waved our thanks to the policeman, took the old 12/50 back to the graveyard and left it there. It had been a timely warning.

While I'd been scared enough when I'd boiled the engine, it was chicken feed compared to what was coming my way. Our safety harness had an unlocking bolt which would flip up to unlatch, thus giving a few inches of freedom to move your head and shoulders for better all-round visibility when taxiing on the ground. Before take-off you relocked it, of course. But that day I forgot.

It was a solo aerobatic exercise, and I'd started a slow roll, but as soon as I got inverted I slid out of the cockpit and dropped those few inches earthwards before my shoulders hit hard into the safety harness. Petrol poured out of the gravity tank in a face-freezing spray, my feet could no longer reach the rudder bar with any realistic degree of control, and my parachute pack had slid up behind my rump, wedging me away from the back-rest. My right hand, still gripping the spade grip of the control column, was joined by the vice-like grip of my left, the only thing capable of giving me the slightest feeling of security. But by clinging on with both hands I was ensuring, of course, that I could not use the only control that would right the aircraft. Sooner or later, I would have to let go.

Then the engine, starved of fuel, banged and backfired its way into silence, the propeller now a visible disc. There was only one way out of it. Timorously, I transferred the grip of my left hand to the security of the cockpit coaming and pulled the stick back to loop out, hoping that I had enough height to do so without incurring Hamilton's wrath. Was it only last week that he'd said, 'Whatever you get up to in the air, don't hit the ground while doing it'? He was going to be damned annoyed with me if they had to scrape me off the deck after this caper.

The airspeed went right off the clock, and as a biplane is held together by wires of differing lengths, thicknesses and tensions, it cannot be ignored when it has outrageously exceeded its maximum permitted speed. It becomes a subsonic harp, the effect now reinforced by a brazen snarl as fuel reached the engine once more, to send the tips of the over-revving propeller supersonic.

If ever a chap needed his mother it was now. I was still half on my back, but at last my parachute had slid back into place, giving me more semblance of control of this headstrong machine. A wood swung into view, and as it passed out of sight, a field, and a stream. I was safe, but only just.

Levelling out a nerve-shattering hundred feet above the ground, I took my howling, snarling machine towards a herd of Friesians peacefully grazing their way into the next pint of milk a few fields ahead. We must have seemed like the Angel of Death to them, in each bovine mind the peaceful image of the milking parlour being replaced by one of the abattoir. They scattered as chaff before the wind and were lost to sight, and I swept upwards to safety, snapping the harness latch into place with shaking fingers.

'Today', said Hamilton, 'we are going to perform "Restarting a Stopped Propeller".' (As we had no self-starting system it would be a serious matter if our only engine stopped in flight.) 'Take her up to 6,000 feet.' There, he closed the throttle, switched off the magnetos, and flat-turned and skidded the machine until the propeller jolted to a halt, its diaphanous disc becoming a stationary piece of yellow wood, our sole means of propulsion. I hoped this trick was going to work.

'The reaction must be immediate, Edwards. Don't ponce around losing height, and as we've had to stop the engine artificially by switching off the magnetos, switch them on again.'

Saying which, he rammed the machine into a near-vertical dive, and I was grateful when my stomach returned to its usual location in my abdomen. The machine went into the usual heavenly-harp routine, the sound level building up as fast as the altimeter needle was winding down. I stared ahead, past that damned useless propeller, and had the feeling that we were on a loser.

'Sir,' I bellowed down the Gosport tubes, 'just to the left of the air intakes is a good field – the one with a pond in it. If we pulled out now I think I could get her down in it.'

I hoped that he could detect the note of pleading in my voice.

'Wait for it, Edwards, wait for it,' roared Hamilton. 'you've got to react the moment the propeller starts.'

' *If* it starts', I muttered.

'I heard that, Edwards. Don't be so bloody bolshie.'

I was leaning to the conclusion that maybe Bolshevism had a lot going for it when a ray of hope appeared: the propeller eased over a fraction to the right.

But it stopped! Then flicked through a half revolution until the 21 litres of dead engine stopped it with a thud that shook the already-suffering airframe. Then it moved again, though with the greatest reluctance, obviously resisting all the way. Then it moved a bit more, before – thankfully – vanishing into invisibility as the engine fired. The rev counter shot wildly into the red despite the closed throttle, Hamilton pulled all the G in the world, and we shot up to 3,000 feet with no effort at all.

'Now don't forget, Edwards. This exercise is only to be carried out under dual instruction.'

As he spoke the engine died, and his voice came down the tubes again. 'OK. That field you were rabbiting on about on the way down. Your engine's failed. Get me down in it.'

'Are there any mushrooms in it, sir?'

'We'll find out when we get there.'

As I flew contentedly home Hamilton interrupted my reverie.

'Edwards, if you ever *do* have a solo crack at that restarting caper, *do* remember to switch on the magnetos again.'

'Yessir.'

But half-way down the dive, with the spires of Shrewsbury enlarging inexorably between the air intakes, I was starting to regret my decision.

The Junior Term drew to a close, and as I was passing the watchtower on one of those leisurely end-of-term days a group of instructors was leaving the Chief Instructor's office, Hamilton among them. He'd been newly promoted to flight lieutenant, so I went over to congratulate him.

'Thank you, Edwards. By the way, I've got your flying assessment here.'

God! I thought of the time I'd nearly baled out after the 'fire', of the unlatched slow roll, of the forbidden restarting of a stopped propeller. Maybe someone *had* seen me after all. But Hamilton was smiling. 'Take a look at it.'

He handed me my flying log-book, and I stared in astonishment at the two statements in it: 'Proficiency as pilot on type – Exceptional. Any special faults in flying which must be watched – None.'

'Congratulations, Edwards. You're my first.'

We went on a fortnight's leave, and I caught up with my

family, and with news of the outside world, that had seemed of lesser importance compared with the world of flying. The Spanish Civil War continued to rage, and once Russia became involved it gave Hitler justification for backing Franco, and a wonderful opportunity to try out the new Messerschmitt 109 fighter that was to bedevil our lives in 1940. My family's only *personal* involvement in Spanish affairs was the border collie dog which my mother had recently acquired, naming him Alfonso after the deposed Spanish King.

On return from leave we were now in the Senior Term, to do applied flying on the Audax, which carried full military equipment, and we were paired off to fly from the front seat as pilot, or in the back cockpit to do gunnery, bomb aiming and camera exercises. I was paired with a New Zealander called Lucas, an elderly 23 from my 18-year-old viewpoint, but we developed a good relationship as we worked at our routines in the air. With fewer instructors to keep tabs on us we now had more freedom of action, and it was an accepted perk that we could shoot lines to the local girls, who often watched the flying by perching on the fence running along the main road. We made our landing approaches as low as we dared without arousing the wrath of our instructors to make the girls jump off the fence in real, or affected, terror. From the back cockpit we blew them kisses, or made gallant comments, though not always. Once I had succeeded in producing a flurry of summer frocks and knickers as the girls got off the fence in a hurry when Luke, leaning far out of the back cockpit, shouted 'What hairy legs' at one up-ended girl. I felt that that was going too far.

A big setback for Germany in 1937 was the loss by fire of their luxury airship *Hindenburg*. Thirty-three people died in the hydrogen inferno as it came in to land in America, so its sister-ship *Graf Zeppelin* was immediately withdrawn from service. We had already given up on these lethal machines, and in any case they were doomed, as the commercial airliner was now capable of longer and longer flights, and, as though to rub it in, three days after *Hindenburg*'s accident press photographs of the crash were flown non-stop across the Atlantic for the European papers.

And soon, Imperial Airways would take a half-ounce letter to Durban for a penny-ha'penny. But even more significant was the joint Imperial Airways/Pan American venture of double transatlantic flights using flying-boats. Day by day, the world was getting smaller, and day by day the RAF was getting larger, new aerodromes being built all over England and, of course, in Germany, too.

In May we all had a holiday for the Coronation of King George VI, and a week or so later I was allowed the fly the hottest fighter in the RAF, the superb Hawker Fury, our first fighter to exceed 200 mph, being threatened with a fate worse than death if I bent it. It handled beautifully.

For the last month of the Senior Term we flew across to Lincolnshire for our final weapons training in bombing and gunnery. Jocelyn du Boulay, an instructor, flew me for my first live-firing of a Lewis gun from the back cockpit, and we were flying at about a hundred feet past the line of targets when a flock of sparrows got up in front of us. With no chance of our avoiding them, they and their corpses hurtled back through the flailing propeller and scattered over the aircraft, one vanishing down a carburettor intake, the engine registering immediate disapproval. Another shattered the windscreen, others hit me remarkably hard blows on the head and body, but of more concern were the holes in the linen fabric of the wings, which started to enlarge as the slipstream tore at them.

'I'm taking this heap home, Edwards. Unload the gun', came down the phones.

He jacked up his seat so as to see over the remains of the windscreen, and we landed safely.

'Well, Edwards,' said du Boulay, as I waited for the post-flight debriefing – for the words of wisdom that would stand me in good stead for the rest of my flying life, 'that's two dozen sparrows that will never fuck and fly again, what!'

When our armament training ended we flew back to Tern Hill, and a very memorable flight it was. Flying as two squadrons of twelve aircraft each, I was in the second one, half a mile behind the leaders, but as we neared home we seemed to be catching them up. At the acrimonious post-mortem afterwards it transpired that the leader wanted us to appear over Tern Hill as one impressive formation of twenty-four, so he'd throttled back to 100 mph to allow us to close the gap. But he hadn't briefed *our* leader, and it looked as though we were going to fly right into them. As it became obvious that this could happen, the leading squadron went to full throttle to try and get away from us, and we in the second squadron throttled back to avoid hitting them. The result was that when we *did* fly into them we were all going at about the same speed, and twenty-four aircraft got into a formidable tangle right over the aerodrome, for all to see. (You may remember that a similar cock-up had happened a couple of millennia before, when a chap called Horatius was guarding a bridge somewhere, those behind crying 'Forward', while those in front cried 'Back'.) As our squadron flew into the leader's, each aircraft exploded into individual action as its pilot saw an opening to safety and went for it. I dived to starboard to avoid chewing the tail off the machine ahead of me, and as my wing lifted over his rudder the wheels of another desperate fellow slid the length of my upper wing, far too close for comfort. My dive continued, but another machine below me was lifting itself up from its own potential collision, the pilot looking steadily away from me at his *own* danger spot. I heaved back on everything, half expecting a tearing impact as my wheels tore into his centre-section. It didn't happen, but it left me in a well-established climbing turn, to find the sky above me darkened by another aircraft climbing similarly, but, alas, not so fast. The way I was heading, his propeller would take me in the cockpit area, and whatever lay below me, it could not be worse than that flailing propeller about to make a pulp of my head. As I shoved the stick forward I looked over my right shoulder, and would have been happier not doing so. Filling my vision, an Audax was diving down on me, the pilot invisible in the shadow of the top wing, but the look of horror on the face of the gunner in the back cockpit was all I needed to initiate my instinctive reaction to prevent him from hitting me amidships – hard back on the stick and full right rudder, knowing in some nagging way that there was something inherently wrong in the action.

It clicked! I was setting up a flick roll, a manoeuvre that an Audax would take at a reasonable speed, say 100 mph, but not at the 150 I'd clocked up. She was going to shed all four wings as soon as the flick developed. Scared stiff, I reversed all controls, and to hell with what lay ahead. But I was already over the vertical, and came round to be carried back into the whirling dance of death.

Then a Fury in a hell of a hurry swept across my nose. By the length of pilot sticking out of its cockpit like an asparagus stalk I knew it was the 6 ft 2 in. Jim Nicolson, in three years' time to earn the only Victoria Cross awarded to a fighter pilot in the Battle of Britain, and five years after that to vanish in the wastes of South-East Asia. I hit Nic's slipstream with a thud, and then I was out in the clear.

'You know, sir,' said my batman as he laid out my mess kit that night, 'that was the most magnificent display of flying I've ever seen. Like the dog-fights of the Great War. All we batmen think that your term are the best fliers who've ever been through Tern Hill.'

I didn't disillusion him that he'd nearly witnessed what would have been the biggest flying accident in the history of the RAF. 'Well, Brittain, we do our best, you know.'

The Armament Practice Camp was the culmination of our training. There was the usual delight of the Passing-Out Parade, with the bands playing as we marched and swaggered on the parade ground, fully fledged acting pilot officers, and no longer on probation. We were on our divergent ways to our squadrons, in my case No. 233 General Reconnaissance Squadron of Coastal Command, whose motto was *Fortis et Fidelis* – Strong and Faithful.

I hoped to be both.

No. 233 was stationed at Thornaby, in Yorkshire, and first impressions were disappointing. The mess and living quarters were a drab collection of wooden huts of First World War vintage, the partitions between the bedrooms being yellow-painted straw-board about an inch thick, insufficient to prevent sounds from passing through. Each room had an iron bedstead, a table and easy chair, a coal scuttle and a chamber pot, the latter much in use by the wealthier when draining the oil from the sumps of their cars. There was also a bookcase, but the room was so small that this had to be put on the table. In one corner was a coal-burning stove, its cast-iron flue backed on two sides by asbestos sheets as a fire precaution. It was practical, but very uncosy.

The aircraft were a disappointment, too. The Anson was a hastily modified small civil airliner designed for economical operation, and was under-powered for a military aircraft. By the time they'd put two machine-guns and the rest of the equipment into it, the weight of bombs that it would carry was a pathetic 280 lb. It was, however, a technological advance, being a monoplane, though this was viewed with suspicion by the more conservative of us, as it lacked the wires which you could *see* were holding a biplane together. It also had a retractable undercarriage, though this had to be laboriously wound up and down by hand. But a big bonus was that it was fitted with the new six-instrument blind-flying panel, a real advance in air safety.

Just as our Anson was the product of the RAF's rapid expansion programme, so were the personnel. We had only two experienced officers, our CO, Sqn Ldr Wallis, and Flt Lt 'Monty' Banks, who commanded 'A' Flight. The remaining pilots, both officers and sergeants, had all left their flying training schools within the last two months. Similarly, in the ground crews a few experienced NCOs were in charge of the newly qualified tradesmen who serviced our aircraft. We were 150 vastly inexperienced men, and were fortunate in having two years in which to get ready for war, though when it did start in September 1939 we still had our woefully inadequate Ansons. And people kept forgetting to wind the undercarriage down for the landing, resulting in the propellers being bent into shapes that would have inspired Salvador Dali. This expensive pastime was countered by mounting a klaxon horn a foot from the pilot's left ear, which went into unmistakable action if the throttles were closed when the wheels were still up. But a disadvantage was that in a steep descent, as in cloud, with the throttles closed, it nearly drove you demented, so a modification was introduced by some pilots. In their fury they reached out and ripped off the electrical leads, the descent then being continued in perfect peace. After landing the pilot would tell the electrician to reconnect it.

Only sometimes he didn't. And it could start all over again.

We shared the station with the equally inexperienced 224 Squadron, and had to start from scratch to learn our role of maritime reconnaissance. Increasingly complex navigation exercises were held, at first over land, but later exclusively over the sea, but the wireless sets rarely worked properly, as our operators were even less experienced, relatively, than we were as pilots and navigators, and this led to a great deal of strain in bad weather, when the radio bearings so essential to safety were frequently not forthcoming. It took its toll. In the next eighteen months thirteen people died in three crashes, one of them being Monty Banks, our only flight lieutenant, leaving the CO with no officer above the rank of pilot officer.

These deaths introduced us to a service custom that seemed at first sight to be heartless – that of auctioning off the deceased's kit to his brother officers. The thinking behind it was that the parents of an officer could be well off, and would have no use for many of the service items, whereas some junior officers were struggling, and could do with cheap ways of making up their kit. With the next-of-kin's permission the auction would take place in the anteroom, and would start with the CO's statement that high bids were not essential, an indication that the parents did not need the money, or a hint to the contrary, in which case the bidding would be high. I bought a few things at one of these auctions as I wasn't all that well equipped myself.

At the sales of a dead aircraftman's kit, however, the prices were almost always high, as the likelihood was that the parents or widow would need the money. It was very touching to hear of an AC2, the lowest-paid man in the service, bidding the new price for an oil-stained tunic that he couldn't wear without first paying for it to be dry-cleaned, unless he relished a rollicking from his disciplinary Flight Sergeant. Frequently, after being bought, the item would be tossed back for resale. It was an indescribable aspect of service life that would never obtain in Civvie Street.

The large industrial complex of Teesside poured out smoke and pollution, and when flying northwards even fifty miles out to sea we knew when we were off the Tees, as the visibility would steadily deteriorate, and even the smells would be detectable. In early 1938 I was navigating 'Hoppy' Hopkins in such an area, but as we flew further up the Tees estuary on our way home things got so bad that Hoppy decided to force-land in a farmer's field. As was customary, people sprang out of the ground from nowhere, and it became a social occasion. But we had to let the squadron know that we weren't at the bottom of the sea, and so, successfully ignoring the kindly suggestion of a middle-aged man that we could use his phone, we opted for the obviously more convenient one offered by a couple of teenage girls. Having rung the squadron, we swigged the cups of tea on offer from their parents, and mightily impressed our captive audience with tales of the perils and excitement of RAF life. By the time we'd eaten the lunch so kindly on offer the weather had cleared, and the girls came along to see us off. And I rather wished they hadn't, as Hoppy, being captain, sat in state in the cockpit putting on his daredevil act, while I had to slave my guts out on the engine-winding handles, an undignified procedure.

The rank of squadron commander was upgraded, and Wg Cdr Lewis George le Blount Croke took over. Louis was an impressive six-foot-plus, big built and with a large hooked nose. Ex-Navy, he gave the impression that he had been trained in sail, his voice at full throttle being impressive, easily heard above the noise of a Force 8 gale. He arrived with several good ideas, one being that as the Navy did a spring cruise each year a maritime reconnaissance squadron should do the same. He organised a four-day exercise that would take us from Thornaby as far north as Skerryvore off the west of Scotland, as far south as Manston in Kent, and as far to the east as the Haaks light-vessel off the Dutch coast. When away from land we would drop aluminium-dust sea markers as targets for practice bombing and machine-gun fire, the whole thing taking a great deal of planning.

The day before the exercise started Goering announced to the people of Austria that their economic life would be amalgamated with that of Germany, and went on:

'I must address a serious warning to the city of Vienna, which can no longer be called a German city because there are 300,000 Jews. We do not want the Jews, neither in the cultural nor economic spheres, and their elimination must be carried out systematically. I instruct the *Reichstathalter* of Austria to take, with all care and within the law, but without clemency, those measures which are necessary for the elimination of the Jews from business, and for the Aryanisation of trade and business.'

Chilling and merciless words, and only a small measure of what was to come, did we but know it.

The day after that dreadful speech, 233's spring cruise of twelve Ansons took to the air, flying a complicated exercise involving five changes of track out to sea, and landing at Abbotsinch, near Glasgow, where, in typical British fashion, the weather closed down, and we had to stay the night. The Station Navigation Officer worked like mad to rearrange the complicated schedule, and we got off the next day for a trip round the light-vessels of the English Channel, returning to Bircham Newton in Norfolk. The next day we did a four-hour stint out to the Haaks lightship off the Dutch coast before coming home again. It had all been a great success – no aircraft had gone unserviceable, and few problems had been encountered. It was undoubtedly a feather in Louis' cap.

In the mess that night, 224, our brother squadron, no doubt smarting under our success, started getting uppity.

'I've got just the thing for putting this bunch in their place', I said to my Flight Commander. (A month or two back I'd blued half a week's pay on a cased pair of 1815 flintlock duelling pistols, tests confirming that they were fully functional.) I explained.

'Duelling pistols! You can't fire guns in the *mess*! Two two four certainly deserve it, but you can't start shooting the buggers.'

'Just blank charges, old boy. Lots of noise and lots of smoke. It'll scare the hell out of them.'

'Good idea.'

After the first thunderous discharge a stunned silence descended on the anteroom. Then a 224 type yelled, 'The bastard's crazy, get him.'

This was easier said than done, as I had retired behind the protection of 233 to reload, and the next discharge persuaded them that we had the upper hand.

'All right, we capitulate', said 'Dogshooter' Wimperly. 'Just buy me a pint to wash that bloody powder smoke out of my throat.'

Dogshooter was a keen sporting shot, and had acquired his nickname as a result of an unfortunate misjudgement in the shooting field. Firing at a low-flying pheasant – which he shouldn't have done, even if it *was* behind the line of guns – he'd slightly peppered a picker-up dog, who came howling out of the bushes, more surprised than injured. While Dogshooter had lived it down in the shooting world, he had not been allowed to in the RAF, and he was a bit sensitive about it.

However, I soon became a victim of such an insensitive system myself. The squadron had been to see Walt Disney's *Snow White and the Seven Dwarfs*, but I was Orderly Officer, so couldn't go. On return a group of them came over in the anteroom and seemed to examine me at length.

'You're right', said Robinson to Derbyshire. 'Just turn your head a little to the right, Edwards.'

'What on earth for?'

'Small thing to ask. Just do it.'

I obliged.

'Yes, spot on. You see, Edwards, Derbyshire here thinks that you look just like Dopey, one of the seven dwarfs.'

'Oh, thank you much, Derbyshire. Most grateful, I'm sure.'

'Come on, Dopey, it's not so bad. And you *do* fire off pistols in the mess, you know. They don't come much crazier.'

It rankled. After I'd finished my Orderly Officer duties that night I loaded the pistols and opened the door of Derbyshire's room. 'You asleep, Derbyshire?'

'I was until you burst in.'

'Look, do you *really* think I look like Dopey?'

'Yeah. Spitting image.'

I fired the first pistol, the flame of its discharge lighting up the room as it boomed out.

'My God, you crazy bastard!'

'Still think so?'

'Yes ... I mean NO', he corrected, too late. The priming of the second pistol was already burning, and the process repeated itself. I shut the door on the room and its sulphurous fumes and got back into bed. Then I thought better of it, reloaded the pistols and went back.

'Still awake, Derbyshire?'

'Fuck off.'

I fired both together, and hoped he'd asphyxiate in the fumes.

'For God's sake leave the poor bugger alone', came Robinson's protest through the one-inch strawboard partition. 'Get off to bed. And if you come anywhere near me with those pistols, Dopey, you'll get my boot in your crutch.'

It looked as though I was stuck with the name.

A few weeks later came the final stage of flight training. Along with several others I was detached to Thorney Island, near Portsmouth, for the navigation/reconnaissance course. Here we practised various types of search and patrol patterns, code and cipher systems were mastered, and ship recognition rammed into us, it being essential to recognise not only all Royal Navy vessels, but also those of our potential allies the French, and our probable enemies, the Germans and Italians.

I thought it to be a merely academic matter, but we also learned the ships of the American Navy, and I was pleased, on one of our navigation exercises, to find three of their battleships sailing up the Solent, easily recognisable by their lattice-type mainmasts. I sent a hasty sighting report back to base, hoping that my course tutor would realise what a bright spark he had on his hands.

Thorney Island was a pleasant place in which to relax off

duty. We roamed the coast from Chichester to Portsmouth, picnicked on the South Downs, lying out in the sun and watching the butterflies on their erratic flights. And four of us clubbed together and bought an elderly centre-board sailing dinghy, sailing up and down the sheltered waters of Chichester harbour.

As the summer passed we learned that both 233 and 224 Squadrons had moved from Thornaby to Leuchars on the east coast of Scotland, a popular move from the reports that filtered back to us. In the mounting international tension over Germany's pressure on Czechoslovakia the navigation/reconnaissance course ended, and I made the long trip north to my squadron in Scotland.

Chapter Two

Reinforcing the Raj

I arrived from Thorney Island to find both squadrons happily
settled at Leuchars, a well-established station on the east
coast of Scotland five miles out of St Andrews. But no sooner
had I arrived than the Czechoslovakian crisis teetered on the
edge of war, and our maritime reconnaissance squadron moved
thirty miles up the coast to its war station at Montrose, so as to
be that little bit nearer to Norway, though with our inadequate
Ansons we still couldn't get there.

Montrose was a Flying Training School, and couldn't cope
with the influx of a couple of hundred men and twenty-four
aircraft, so for living quarters we took over a disused factory.
Field kitchens were delivered, palliasses arrived, and a local
farmer delivered the straw to stuff them as our beds. My
penchant for the use of flintlock pistols at mess parties had
caused the CO to consider that it would be better for all
concerned if I sublimated my urges, and I had been appointed
Squadron Armament Officer. I was kept busy overseeing the
stripping, cleaning and remounting of all our Vickers and Lewis
guns. Then my bombs and ammunition started to arrive, and as
Montrose – a non-operational unit – had no bomb dump, I led a
dog's life finding places to store tons of high explosive in a
station not equipped for it. I'd find a likely spot when no one
was looking, bring along my three-ton trucks and unload their
lethal cargo, covering it up with tarpaulins. But as often as not
some wrathful Montrose senior officer would be baying for my
blood within the hour, with some such trifling complaint as that
I had dumped umpteen tons of high explosive within six feet of
the main electricity cable supplying the camp.

One wartime requirement caused distress to all the

squadron. Our Ansons were painted silver, with the squadron crest in enamel paints on the fins, and very elegant they looked. We were told to scrape these crests right off, so that we could not be identified if we were shot down over enemy territory, though how we could ever reach enemy territory, except by rail, defeated us. That done, we had to camouflage them in the modern drab brown and green, and our pretty silver Ansons disappeared for ever.

Then the Prime Minister brought back that useless piece of paper from Munich, and the crisis was over. We all went home to Leuchars, where we were still allowed to take aircraft away on weekend leave, a boon for those of us living well to the south. This wasn't the indulgent waste of taxpayers' money that you might think, as the flights were treated as navigation exercises, and the logs had to be handed in to the Navigation Officer for analysis on return. Sealand, near Chester, was my weekend aerodrome, as it was only ten miles from my home in North Wales. My eldest brother worked in Mold, and possessed an elderly and sluggish Austin 10 that couldn't have pulled the skin off a rice pudding. I would fly low over his office, my infringement of the low-flying regulations being looked upon tolerantly as I was the only pilot for miles around, and anyway my grandfather was Chairman of the Magistrates. Alerted by the engine noise, my brother would come out into the office courtyard and give me the 'thumbs up', after which I would fly off to Sealand. By the time I'd refuelled and accommodated the aircraft, he would have arrived at the tarmac to collect me, in a door-to-door service.

I returned the gesture on Monday morning by telling the Duty Pilot that I was having magneto trouble on one engine, and would need to do a local check flight before undertaking the long and arduous trip to Scotland. I would then render my brother invisible by dressing him up in my Teddy bear Sidcot suit, and fly him low over our village. Knowing the local topography well, I could put up quite a show, slipping into the valley a mile from home and staying at about fifty feet, out of sight. At the last minute I'd pull the stick back and, with a roar of mighty engines, rise as though from the very earth itself. It was all very good for one's ego.

On such trips we also discovered what an enormous number of new aerodromes were being built up and down the country, and it was quite a problem keeping our maps up to date. On one occasion I was going to Sealand as usual, but would divert to drop off Ali Barber, my navigator, at Abingdon, near Oxford. The weather report was adequate for Sealand, but doubtful for the Oxford area, and as we flew southwards in deteriorating weather I became uneasy, but Ali reassured me.

'Don't worry, Dopey. I know Abingdon like the back of my hand. We'll get in OK.'

But it was now snowing, and the reduced visibility made things unpleasant and unsafe. As Ali and I strained our vision forwards we had no time to be astounded as, in a one in a billion chance, a twin-engined Oxford trainer on an exactly reciprocal course, and only twenty feet or so above us, hurtled out of the snow and shot over our roof like a bullet. Our combined 300 mph slipstreams hit with a bang that hammered our Anson into a vibrating mass of wood and metal. In the front, Ali and I had had that split second's warning of the bang, but our other passengers had none, and it was very frightening for them. Ali and I saw the funny side, and howled with laughter, watched by a hostile audience.

Then a thought struck me.

'Ali, it wasn't all *that* bloody funny. I'm turning back for Sealand: you'll have to catch a train from Chester.'

'Catch a train!' bawled Ali, the near-miss instantly forgotten. 'And miss what's laid on for me! I tell you, that girl's got tits like jellies on springs. There's no problem, Dopey, I'll get you into Abingdon. Trust me.'

Foolishly, I did.

'We'll get over the centre of Oxford first', said Ali.

The snow changed to sleet as I flew ever lower to keep clear of the cloud base, some of the dreaming spires waking up with a start as we flashed past not very many feet above their weathercocks.

'OK. Follow that railway line.'

I did a split-arse turn.

'Now here's the crossroads. Turn right at the garage.'

No garage appeared.

'Funny,' said Ali, 'but don't worry, the transport café will turn up soon.'

It didn't.

'Look, Ali, you don't know you arse from your elbow. Admit it.'

'Admit nothing. What d'you think that is?'

He pointed ahead, where the aerodrome was becoming visible in the murk.

'Abingdon, spot on.'

He spun the wheels down, and we landed in a flurry of heavy snow, which reduced the visibility even more. Then, out of the murk, appeared an unusual object for a grass aerodrome – a stake of wood three feet high, which some clot of a surveyor had probably knocked into the ground and forgotten to remove. With no chance of avoidance it vanished under the port wing, and there was a jolt as the entire port tailplane ripped off.

My weekend at home had vanished.

But at least we were still in time for lunch in the mess, where, across the table, Ali spotted a chap called Waterhouse who'd been at Flying Training School with him.

'Hi, Closet,' bellowed Ali in his usual loud voice, 'nice to see you again. But I always thought you were at Harwell.'

'I *am*', said Waterhouse in the unfortunate silence which happened to occur at that particular moment. 'So are *you*.'

The hush that had fallen on the dining room lasted fully a second before the bomber boys fell about laughing at the standard of Coastal Command's navigation. I slunk out in shame and went down to Flights, where I dug out the Servicing NCO.

'What d'you make of this lot, Chiefy?'

'Firewood, sir. You'll need a new tailplane.'

'How long's that going to take?'

'Difficult to tell, sir. We're a Bomber Command Group and don't fly Ansons. I'll have to find a Maintenance Unit that stocks Anson spares, then find a carpenter rigger. We haven't got one as our Hinds are all-metal. Then a day to fit it. And it's Friday afternoon, sir.'

I rang 233's Adjutant.

'Dai, I'm stuck at Harwell with a broken tailplane. God knows when I'll get home, but it's going to be at least four days. Will you break the news to the CO?'

'No way. *You* tell him. You *do* remember, don't you, that you signalled that you'd landed at Abingdon. No, the ball's in your court, Dopey. I'm putting you through to Wing Commander Lewis George le Blount Croke, and God help you, mate.'

God was unsupportive. While acknowledging that I couldn't fly without a tailplane, Louis hinted that it would be better for my promotion prospects if the job could be done in the next few minutes.

The days went past. Ali Barber rang in each morning against a background of creaking bedsprings. My money ran out, and I was bored rigid. At last a low-loader arrived with my new tailplane, which was fitted within the day. I rang the CO with the good news.

'Right, Edwards. I'll see you tomorrow.'

Which just goes to show how mistaken you can be.

In doubtful weather we got airborne, and within a quarter of an hour the radio had packed in. Deeper and deeper into the murk I flew, until Louis' wrath counted for naught. By the skin of my teeth I scraped in to the Yorkshire aerodrome of Dishforth, and rang Dai Davies again.

'Guess where we are, Dai?'

'Not Leuchars, that's for sure. Louis's going to be *so* disappointed. And the weather forecast for the next few days is awful – you're not going to be able to fly. *Do* let me put you through.'

'EDWARDSSSS!'

'Sir.'

'Catch the train.'

'Catch the *what*, sir?'

But he'd already put the phone down.

By the time we'd made the miserable journey north Louis had cooled down a bit, but the bad weather held for three more days, after which Dai Davies managed to get out of his

Adjutant's office for a breath of fresh air and flew me down to Dishforth. Twelve days after leaving Leuchars on a three-day weekend, K8815, with her spanking new tailplane, was back in the roost.

But in the nationwide bad weather two others of our weekend aircraft had also been stuck away for several days, and Louis became more cautious in his future interpretation of weekend weather reports.

However, active as ever, now that we were in Scotland he started a pipe band. Known pipers were posted from units in Bomber and Fighter Commands, and a piper was located down at Gosport.

I was ordered to collect him, and as I fired up the port engine Louis seemed to have doubts as to my suitability for so important a mission, clambering aboard and saying, 'Get him inside the aircraft as soon as you land and don't let him go, or I'll have your guts for garters.'

He left, and I fired up the starboard engine.

Louis returned to the cockpit. 'Make sure he knows how to use his parachute.'

As I completed the magneto checks and moved away from the tarmac, Louis waved me to a halt. Through the open side-window, and above the noise of the clattering engines came the final bellowed instruction: 'If he *does* have to bale out make sure he takes his bagpipes with him.'

The band took shape, and improved greatly when a retired pipe major was discovered to be living just down the estuary. Subscriptions towards the band were asked for from the officers, and who could resist those melting blue eyes – or was it that great hooked nose and the power of life and death that Louis had over us? We paid up.

When the Pipe Major was entertained in the mess I formed the opinion that his bagpipe differed from those of the run-of-the-mill pipers as it seemed to need inflation by pure whisky fumes, our subscriptions obviously helping to support this habit. He drank, of course, only the most expensive single malts.

But it was all worth it, and the day dawned when the band was considered fit to perform at the 08.30 parade, not only for our squadron to hear, but for the whole station. Before we marched off the parade ground the band went into the usual squeal-and-howl start-up routine, and then got going. If ever pipes skirled it was our mob. It was magnificent! A Celt myself, though from gentler climes, it fired my blood, and even that of the hitherto lukewarm Sassenachs who formed the bulk of the squadron. First we marched, then we strutted, and when the sound really got into our bloodstreams we *swaggered* to work. It was magnificent!

We celebrated that night by bringing two motorbikes into the mess, where a broad central corridor was crossed at intervals by lateral ones leading to the bedrooms. One bike did runs up and down the main corridor while the other did chicken runs across it. The bikes rarely collided, but I felt it would be safer if there was a starting system, so went to my quarters, loaded up my duelling pistols, and brought some reloads with me.

The crash of the first shot stopped everyone in their tracks, enabling me to explain the new starting system, after which things really took off, until the anteroom door swung open to reveal, just discernible through the gun smoke, the Station Adjutant in his pyjamas and dressing-gown.

Despite his lack of height, Chota White was a formidable character, his great weakness being a tiresome insistence on placing people under arrest when he was tight, which was often. (He was one of the many lonely survivors of the Great War.) Fortunately, his memory was of short duration when he was in this state, so the arrested officer would leave the room, wait a minute or two, and return via another door, by which time Chota would have forgotten the incident.

But this time he was obviously livid at being aroused from his beauty sleep. He took a deep, fume-laden breath and laid into us. The motorbikes were heaved out of the mess, and then he spotted my duelling pistols.

'As for you, Edwards, you're under arrest. Go to your room.'

I left the anteroom, used the statutory pause to reload the pistols, and returned through the door by which Chota had come in. He was still giving the chaps the rough end of his tongue as I crept up behind him and fired the first pistol. As his

empurpled face reappeared through the smoke like an enraged
– if rather small – bull elephant, he was obviously on the verge
of apoplexy. But far worse, he was sober. Stone cold sober. And
shaking with rage. 'Edwards, I told you that you were under
arrest. Go immediately to your room or I'll send you there under
escort', he roared. 'And I'm confiscating those pistols. Hand
them over.'

'Well, actually Chota, one of them is still loaded.'

'Well actually, Edwards, fire the damned thing off then.'

I squeezed the trigger as deferentially as possible, but in its
entirely undeferential way it went off. As soon as Chota
reappeared through the gunsmoke I handed him the pistols and
went to my room.

In the morning I took vows that never again would I combine
alcohol, exhaust fumes and gun smoke to quite the same extent.
The anteroom, as I passed through on my way to breakfast,
stank of fumes and was littered with the shredded newspaper
wadding of my pistols. I thanked my lucky stars that the Station
and Squadron Commanders were all married, and living out of
mess, as they'd cashier the lot of us if they saw the state of that
room. As I carried on into the dining room Chota White
exploded as soon as he saw me.

'Don't you know you're under arrest? Go back to your room
immediately, and stay there until I send for you.'

Back in my room I sent for Brittain, my batman. He'd been in
the Marines, so would know a thing or two.

'Brittain, I'm under arrest.'

'Oh, I'm sorry to hear that, sir. Is it serious?'

I explained.

'Have you got your *King's Regulations*, sir?'

'Over there.'

He riffled through the ages before saying 'I think that there
are three main charges that could be levelled against you, sir –
Conduct unbecoming an officer and a gentleman; Disgraceful
behaviour in a professional respect; and Conduct prejudicial to
the maintenance of good order and discipline.'

'Nothing, Brittain, under "Firing, when under arrest, a pair of
flintlock pistols near the earhole of a Station Adjutant on the

only night of the year when the latter was sober?"'

'Nothing, sir.'

There was a hammering on the door, and Robinson of C Flight barged into the room.

'Prisoner, attennnnSHUN. Right turn, quick march, left wheel …'

'Oh, shut up, Rob. What do you want?'

'Well, some Alka-Seltzer wouldn't go amiss, but Chota wants to see you, and I'm your escort. Don't make a bolt for it or I'll be in the shit too. I'm still half deaf from those bloody pistols of yours.

'Sorry, Rob.'

At Station HQ Rob was dismissed, and I stood quivering to attention as Chota continued signing forms and reading letters, a fairly normal softening-up process. Eventually he looked up, ominously addressing me by my surname.

'Edwards, the discharge of firearms in the mess is an act of gross irresponsibility, but more serious is that you disobeyed a reasonable order to consider yourself under arrest – *King's Regulations* Paragraph 1234567 (ii) (d).' He tapped the open volume on his desk. 'That charge merits my referring you to the Station Commander.'

Through the communicating door the Group Captain could be heard stirring. I prayed that he wouldn't come in.

'The annual recommendations for promotion are due at the end of this month, and I must consider whether or not yours should be deferred until you show a greater degree of responsibility.'

'Chota! Sorry. Sir. You wouldn't do a thing like that!'

'I'll do anything I like, you insubordinate puppy, commensurate with the gravity of the offence.'

Puppy! Commensurate! Gravity! Chota was on his high horse.

The bell on his desk rang, and he went into the Groupie's office. As the minutes dragged by I hoped I wasn't featuring in the conversation. Loss of promotion was bad enough, but the loss of cash wouldn't be much fun either, as I was sending some home to my mother each month.

After a long absence Chota came back, seeming very

preoccupied. He sat down and looked at me as though for the first time that morning.

'What do *you* want, Dopey?'

'Er, nothing, sir. It was you who wanted *me*.'

'Oh yes. So it was. Look, these pistols.' He picked them up from his desk. 'If you ever fire these damned things in my lughole again I'll bury my foot so deep in your arse that it'll take half your precious squadron to pull it out again. Now get off to work.'

I'd got off lightly. I took the pistols and left.

Chota *had* taken the matter no further. In June my promotion to flying officer came through, and I was now being paid about seven pounds a week. A month or so previously the national wage for railwaymen was approved at 43 shillings a week, a claim by the National Union of Railwaymen for a minimum wage of 50 shillings being rejected out of hand, of course.

We were fortunate in that Gp Capt Baker had stayed on as Station Commander when the squadrons took over, as most of the social contacts with the local people were retained, a complete contrast to Thornaby, where we had been an island of servicemen dumped in an indifferent industrial environment. The mess was warm and comfortable, though the messing charge was high. In the services a living ration was supplied daily for each man, but as this was pretty basic fare officers elected to pay extra on their mess bills for modest luxuries, chiefly in the food line, but perhaps for decoration or furnishing of the mess. The standard charge in most messes was 3s 6d a day – about 17p – but at Leuchars we paid 3s 9d, the extra thruppence making for a noticeable difference in the luxury of the mess.

There was to be a mess party to introduce us to the local community, and we all voted half a day's pay towards the cost. First and foremost was that we had to learn Scottish country dancing, an instructress visiting the mess to put us through our paces. This was great fun, especially the whooping and hopping around in such things as the Eightsome Reel and Dashing White Sergeant, for which 233's pipe band would play. Flowers were ordered and invitations went out, local people volunteering to put long-distance travellers up for a couple of days. Cross-country flights were planned for purposes not too closely investigated, and we were lectured by the CO on looking after wallflowers. 'If I see *one* girl sitting by herself against a wall I'll know where to look for my Orderly Officers for the next month', said Louis.

The great day came. Early in the morning several aircraft took off on 'navigation exercises', the squadrons' silver was laid out and flowers were strewn around. The aircraft returned from their exercises, discharging one or two rather long-haired passengers wearing anonymous Sidcot suits.

By 19.30 hours a glossy array of well-scrubbed officers accepted a sherry from the kid-gloved hands of the mess waiters.

'Now, don't forget, you lot,' said Chota White, 'this is a public relations party, not a squadron piss-up. It's sherry till the guests arrive, not beer. This isn't the bloody NAAFI.'

'No, sir. I mean yes, sir.'

The party was a great success, many of us bachelors meeting the girls and their families who were to make our time at Leuchars such a happy one. I met Jane, who was, she informed me, at something called the Slade. Whatever the Slade was, it must have been a highly sophisticated organisation, as she ordered a Dry Martini.

'An American drink, I understand, sir', said the barman with an air disapproval that such a drink had got north of the border. 'What they call a cocktail, I believe.'

'That's right. Er, McGarry, have you any idea what the Slade is?'

'God, Dopey,' said Guy Robinson queuing alongside me at the bar, 'you *are* a pleb. It's a fancy art school in London.'

'Thanks, Rob. Got any tips on chatting up a popsie in the art world?'

'Well, there's that chap called Picasso, of course. Just painted a thing called Guernica about the Spanish Civil War. Haven't you seen it? I can't tell the eyes from the arseholes of most of the figures, but that's modern art, of course. Talk about oils, gouache and all that sort of stuff.'

Within a week I had my feet under the table at the hospitable house of Jane's parents, and started an association with the family that would last fifty years.

A few weeks later I travelled down to Woodford, near Manchester, to collect a new Anson from the manufacturers. The aircraft was waiting for me on the tarmac, but so far hadn't been test-flown.

'Won't keep you long', said Bill Thorne, Avro's Chief Test Pilot. He climbed to about 1,500 feet, then appeared to be in serious trouble, as the Anson rolled over onto its back.

'My God! Whatever's happened?' I thought.

But fortunately, it carried on to come the right way up again, and by this time I'd caught on to the fact that it was a well-executed slow roll. Bill followed it with a half loop, and rolled off the top of it. Here was one of these new-fangled monoplanes, *twin-engined* for heaven's sake, and with a wooden wing, still in one piece after aerobatics.

'OK, she's all yours', said Bill after he landed. 'Sign here.'

'Before I sign, Bill, do you do that to all your Ansons?'

I thought maybe he had it in for me.

'Of course; it's a standard part of the test flight.'

I carried the story back to the squadron, and got the impression that, to a man, they approved of the ancients' habit of executing the bearer of bad tidings.

'You say he *rolled* your Anson!' said McKenzie! 'What sort of roll? Not, for God's sake, a flick roll?'

'Well, more like a cheese and onion roll, really.'

'Oh, *very* funny. Now what sort of roll *was* it?'

'Just a slow roll, Donald.'

'Just a slow roll, the gentleman says', continued McKenzie. 'I can tell you what's going to happen next time someone flies into serious turbulence – he's going to end up with a couple of bags of sawdust.'

There it was again – the wisdom of generations handed down from father to son.

I wanted to have a go myself, but a well-executed slow roll is a complex manoeuvre, and it was over a couple of years since

I'd done aerobatics. Then Peter, a new boy straight from Flying Training School, was posted to 'B' Flight. I offered him a deal where he was to gen me up on aerobatics in return for the kudos of being one of the first two squadron pilots to aerobat an Anson. He agreed, with one sensible proviso – we were to wear our parachutes. (In multi-engined aircraft we wore only the parachute harness, the parachute pack itself being stowed in a quick-release rack. When required, it was clipped onto hooks on the front of the harness.) I flew well away from Leuchars and hid behind the largest cumulus cloud I could find. We clipped on the parachute packs, and I found that although it got in the way a bit it didn't seem to interfere with my ability to control the aircraft, an incorrect assumption as it turned out. Peter refreshed me on the complications of the slow roll, but I started with the easiest manoeuvre – a loop. Diving to pick up 165 knots, I hauled firmly back on the stick. She rose nicely into the loop, but as we passed the vertical the control column came into hard contact with the parachute pack on my chest, and would come back no further. We were about 30 degrees inverted when the Anson stalled on its back. We fell off the top of the loop like a ton of bricks, the wooden wings creaked their displeasure, and the speed went off the clock.

God! Was it only a few weeks ago that McKenzie had pointed out that sawdust doesn't fly! We plunged earthwards to the shrieking of the slipstream, and completed a loop that wasn't quite out of the textbook.

'That was a bad idea of yours, Peter.'

'Of *mine?* Yours, you mean.'

'No, not the loop: the parachutes. Off with them.'

The next couple of loops were a doddle, then Peter ruined it all.

'Have you taken a look at the gyro horizon?' he asked.

'Not recently. Why? Oh hell!'

That expensive instrument hadn't taken kindly to being looped, the horizon itself cowering up in the top-left corner of the dial.

'Gosh, Peter, we're nabbed.

'Yes. I think you are.'

I set off unhappily for home.

'D'you think five bob to the instrument repairer would fix things after we land?'

'Well, Dopey, it looks a darned expensive job to me. Ten bob would be nearer the mark.'

Ten bob! Half a day's pay! It was beginning to look like an armoured-car job. The armoured cars of the RAF were one of the major peace-keeping forces in Mesopotamia, backing up on the ground the air action that kept the warring tribesmen from cutting each other's, and our, throats. They also served a secondary purpose as a school of correction for pilots who had blotted their copybooks in one way or another – pranged aircraft, been insubordinate, fired guns in the mess, etc. A couple of years on armoured cars were usually enough to cause the miscreant to mend his ways. Anyone who had done time on them was suspected to have boobed at some time in his career.

But in the event, it didn't cost me a penny, and I never served in armoured cars. By the time we got home the artificial horizon had recovered, and re-erected itself.

'War Games' were now becoming increasingly common. In the last two years we had worked up to a fair degree of skill in our maritime reconnaissance role, and now we also practised fighter affiliation, and with the hitherto hush-hush Hawker Hurricane, a real revelation to us. With a top speed of 330 mph, and with *eight* machine-guns, it made us realise what we might have to face as intruders if war ever came.

Our preparation for attacks on enemy shipping was improved when a high-speed launch with an armoured deck, capable of withstanding our 11½ practice bombs, was delivered to the Marine Section at Newport, on the River Tay. It would go a few miles out to sea and await the arrival of the aircraft, and for this particular exercise I was teamed up with Donald McKenzie. On such a turn-and-turnabout local exercise I don't think we ever bothered to sort out just who was captain of the aircraft, the loose assumption being that whoever was doing the flying at the time was captain.

As wireless communication was not all that reliable in those days, the launch carried back-up smoke signals. As soon as the crew were all snugged up below decks they would light a white smoke candle, but unbeknown to us this time, they'd been having carburettor trouble on both engines, and the fitter was tinkering with things below decks while the rest of the crew lay about dragging on their Woodbines. As we approached, the fitter did a diagnostic start-up of both engines, which gave out great belches of smoke, mistaken by Donald, who was piloting at the time, as the 'OK to bomb' signal. He gave me the go-ahead, and I dropped a real humdinger on our sitting target. Had it been a high-explosive bomb he'd have been blown out of the water.

The reaction of the crew was immediate. Deciding not to finish their Woodbines, they dived below, slammed shut the armoured hatch, and told the engine fitter to tread on it, the engines still pouring out enough smoke for us to mistake it as their willingness to be bombed.

As, like an aerial sheepdog, we hounded our twisting and evasive quarry up the Tay estuary, the smoke died way as the engine fitter got on top of things. It was replaced by a thick trail of unmistakable red smoke, the emergency signal to stop bombing. Alas, my final bomb was on its way, and a mile below us the dinky-toy launch turned into the Marine Section at Newport at a speed that I would have considered to be foolhardy had I been its commanding officer,

Probably the most valuable trait in aircrew is the ability to make instant, correct, decisions, and I made one then. I remembered that it was Donald McKenzie who was captain of the aircraft, his broad shoulders being far more suitable than mine for carrying the can that was undoubtedly coming our way when we landed.

Early in 1939 the outdated biplanes flown by Middle East Command were to be replaced with the new Blenheim twin-engined bomber, and it was to be Coastal Command crews, well used to flying over long stretches of sea, who would deliver them.

A unit was set up at Thorney Island, near Portsmouth, to

organise Blenheim delivery flights, and the competition to get on them was intense, not only because of the fun of flying out to Egypt, but to do so in a modern machine with all the latest gadgets.

In May I joined No. 10 BDF, commanded by Sqn Ldr Abraham, who, at his first conference, had two bits of bad news for us.

'Egypt will be getting pretty warm now, so you'll all need khaki tropical kit. Other ranks will draw theirs from Main Stores tomorrow, but officers, of course, have to provide their own. You'd better nip in to Gieves' branch in Pompey and get two of each.'

Along with others, I still hadn't got the right side of my Gieves bill, and it seemed a bit much to have to go deeper into the red to fly the King's aircraft out to Egypt for him.

The second bit of bad news was that we would do the trip in two days, not in the three taken by previous flights. After lunch with the French Air Force at Marseilles we would go straight on to Malta for the night. We'd miss out on the sleazy joints to which the French Air Force had taken previous flights. There was a third bit of bad news, but only for me – I was to navigate the leader, not fly.

The richer guys among us dutifully bought their kit from Gieves in Portsmouth, and others had been lucky enough to borrow tropical kit from people in their squadrons who had already been overseas. But those of us who hadn't done either voted for mutiny: we bought nothing, and said nothing about it. We'd go to Egypt in our blues.

The Blenheims were not fully operational, as some of their equipment was to be fitted after their arrival in Egypt. Only my lead aircraft would carry a wireless set, so there would be no communication between aircraft. Indeed, there was even no intercom between crew members. The pilot and navigator were stuck up in the nose, and we carried so much in the way of tools and engine spares, which could only be accommodated between the wing spars, that we were cut off from the wireless operator and fourth crew member in the back. We eventually rigged up a hi-tech endless string device to which we tied messages, the crew pulling them inch by inch to the back, and we pulling them forward when required.

We got away from Thorney Island at 07.35 and set course for Lyon, from where we would turn south down the Rhone valley. I made an accurate landfall after crossing the Channel, but we soon flew into ten-tenths cloud over France, and were forced up to 8,000 feet, where, in typical fashion, our single radio set packed up. I had to tell Sqn Ldr Abraham to alter course to the south on an estimated turning time, not by checking with features on the ground, and when we eventually flew clear of cloud I was now hopelessly lost, not a single feature on the ground relating to anything on the map. Abraham asked for our position, which I couldn't give him.

'Well find yourself, and quick. Get a bearing from Marignane.'

'Can't sir. The radio's on the blink.'

'Then hand me your log, and we'll go over the navigation together.'

'Well, the first leg was OK; we hit the French coast spot on. Now how long did you fly the south-easterly course? This looks very odd. Is your watch OK?'

'I didn't use my watch, sir, I used the dashboard clock.'

He checked with his wrist watch.

'Well, that's accurate enough, but it doesn't tie in with your logged times. You *sure* you used that clock?'

'Yes, sir. There it is', I cried, pointing to it.

'Clock, man. CLOCK! That's the bloody altimeter!'

Oh, my God! So it was. The altimeter was the very latest three-finger job, the third finger being hidden at altitudes below 10,000 feet, and in practice at Thorney Island we'd never flown above two thousand. Seven thousand feet looked very much like nine o'clock, my approximate time for turning south. Having found the error, I started to repair the damage.

'You turned south too early, Edwards, didn't you. *How* early?'

I quailed as I gave him the answer.

'FORTY-THREE MINUTES? Nobody makes that sort of mistake. So where are we?'

'A hundred and thirty miles west of track, sir, and off our maps. But if we carry on south we'll hit the Mediterranean coast, where we can turn east for Marseille.'

'Hasn't it struck you, Edwards, that we may be so far to the west that if there's cloud over the Pyrenees we could fly straight into Spain, where, you may remember, there's a civil war going on. Would you prefer to be attacked by one of Mussolini's CR42s or by that new hot-rod of Hitler's – the Messerschmitt 109?'

'In that case, sir, alter course ten degrees to port.'

'I'm making it twenty degrees, Edwards. I'm not having my arse blown off by a trigger-happy Nazi.'

'Perish the thought, sir. Twenty degrees to port it is. I'll log it as from now.'

'Do that. But *do* put in the correct time, there's a good chap. It's 10.15, Edwards, not 8,250 bloody feet.'

We clawed our way back onto the map, closed up into a tight formation over Marignane to let the *Armée de l'Air* know just how good we were, and landed after four hours in the air.

'What's that?' asked Abraham after lunch as I slid into the cockpit alongside him.

'The altimeter, sir.'

'And that?'

'The clock, sir.'

'Correct. Now Malta's a small island, so do get us there in one go, there's a good chap.'

We flew at 5,000 feet above the blueness of the Mediterranean, which was flecked from horizon to horizon with the white horses blown up by the fresh north-westerly wind which was speeding our passage, and turned left round the southern tip of Sardinia. With the wind now right behind us sped along with a groundspeed of an incredible 220 knots, and the wireless was now working again. I felt so confident of my navigation that I was glad that it was Abraham who was doing the flying – it was far more pleasant looking down at the sea a mile below us. Who knew, perhaps we were flying over the site of Atlantis? Maybe, hundreds of feet below the surface, were the foundations and shards that were all that would remain of a civilisation that would never, in their wildest dreams, have visualised men flying at 250 mph over their land. But flying we were, and a very exciting experience it was.

Then, just to the right of Atlantis, the horizon took on a more defined form, and the months of training at Thorney Island kicked in. It was ships, and naval ships at that. I took a bearing on them and worked out their position, but didn't want to draw Abraham's attention to them just then as I wanted to present him with a *fait accompli*, to impress him and make up for my morning's gaffe. As we drew nearer, the ships materialising out of the haze revealed themselves to be Italian, and a complete battle fleet at that. I made my notes, then tapped Abraham on the sleeve.

'Italian battle fleet, sir, bearing green oh-four-oh.'

'They're naval ships all right. Sure they're Italian?'

'Quite sure, sir. Four battleships, nine cruisers, twelve destroyers and some odds and ends. If you'll fly round them I'll get their course and speed, and more ship details.'

'OK, but we won't buzz them too close. What with them invading Abyssinia and all that, we're not exactly the best of friends.'

I got the initial details which I needed and passed them to the wireless operator on our string-operated intercom:

'To HQ Middle-East Command, Cairo, repeated to HQ Coastal Command, Lee-on-Solent.

From 10 BDF in transit Malta–Mersah Matruh. Italian battle fleet at sea position 13 degrees 15 East, 37 degrees 18 North. Course 315 degrees true, speed 18 knots. Composition 4 Battleships, 9 cruisers, 12 destroyers, 11 others. Amplification follows.'

As Abraham continued to circle, I got down to the details of the amplifying report:

'Further to my previous signal, battleships are 1 Littorio, 3 Cavour; heavy cruisers 3 Zara, 2 Trento; light cruisers 4 Condottieri; destroyers 7 Navigatori, 5 Aviere. 11 others.'

With that job done I could now relax, and appreciate the beauty of this great armada, ranging from the 35,000-ton leviathans down to the darting fifteen-hundred-ton destroyers, all rising and falling, lifting and rolling to the rhythm of their individual types, the swift destroyers thrusting their way through the seas, the cruisers taking it in a more leisurely and dignified way, and the massive battleships in slow, ponderous and enormously impressive style.

'Course for Malta please, Edwards.'

We climbed away, and by 18.37 hours Malta and Gozo rose out of the haze, and we landed at Hal Far.

'Now don't forget, chaps, tropical kit in the morning', said Abraham as we said goodnight.

He wasn't at all pleased to see the mixture of khaki and blues next morning, but there was nothing he could do except to express strong disapproval, which he did in no uncertain manner. He went on to say, 'Now do not forget, everybody, that if you have engine trouble or any other disaster and think you can't make it to Egypt, then you can force-land in Libya. But only if you really have to. You're going to be mighty unpopular if you hand over our latest light bomber for Mussolini's gang to examine.'

We set off on our four-hour flight to Mersa Matruh, and slipped inland when we hit the Egyptian coast, flying eastwards over a harsh landscape – yellow sand and rock stretching for miles to the south of us, but the beaches ahead were a delight. With very light-coloured sand, the colour of the sea ranged from deep blue to very pale, depending on its depth, and the shallows were edged by whiter-than-white surf as far as the eye could see.

We landed at Mersah Matruh, which was an advanced landing ground with few facilities and no mess, and so we were refuelled from four-gallon petrol tins by an Arab crew under an RAF NCO, a laborious business which would probably take a couple of hours, but a very welcome break it was. We borrowed the NCO's truck and drove to a wonderful beach where we were the only people, peeled off and swam. After drying out in the sun we went to the only hotel and lay in lounging chairs, awaiting lunch.

'There's only one thing missing to complete this picture, chaps,' I said, 'it's rough luck on some of you, but I'm only navigating. I'm having a pint of Pimm's No. 1.'

The other two pilots looked uneasily at Abraham, lying contentedly with his eyes closed. He spoke.

'Well, special occasion! Half a pint for the pilots and a pint for the navigators. On me.'

They arrived, and Abraham gave the toast, his own particular brand that we had become used to in our fortnight's acquaintance – 'Cheers frightfully ho, chaps.'

'Cheers frightfully ho, sir.'

Gosh, I thought to myself, can *anything* equal this as a style of living?

We got airborne for the overland run to Ismailia, and I ticked off the villages and promontories as we passed – Sidi Haneish, Ras el Hikmak and the soon-to-be-well-known El Alamein. At Zagazig I said, 'Bradshaw to Ismailia, sir. ETA seventeen-eleven.' ('Bradshaw' was the railway guide, and in those days the names of the railway stations were written in foot-high white letters on a black panel. When lost over land the easiest way of finding yourself was to fly low, read the name of the station, and find it on the map.)

As we passed the pyramids Abraham waved a hand at the Sphinx and observed, 'Awful lot of cads, Napoleon's gunners, you know. When they were here they shot half the nose off that thing for target practice.'

As the silvery streak of the Suez Canal appeared ahead, Nos 2 and 3 tucked their wings into a tight V formation, Abraham went to full throttle, and dived in a low sweep over the aerodrome, before pulling up into a steep climb and waving the two wing men away in a Prince of Wales feathers, a manoeuvre strictly forbidden by those in authority, but tolerated as long as it didn't put other aircraft at risk.

We landed; the late afternoon sun being pleasantly warm, and no problem for those of us in our rebellious blues.

'Congratulations all round', said Abraham when we'd all climbed down. 'We've done the UK to Egypt in thirty-three hours – three hours less than it takes Imperial Airways. It's a record.'

It had been worth sacrificing that night in Marseille.

In the evening I got out of the shower to find my bearer, in his uniform of red fez and white gallabiyeh, searching helplessly through my suitcase for the slightest trace of khaki drill. I explained, with minimal undermining of the British Raj, that not all English milords' finances ran to such luxuries. Goode and Anderson were, no doubt, spinning similar tales to their bearers, so I joined them, and the three of us braved the disapproval of the senior officers as we entered the mess together. But we brought fresh news from home, and our blues were soon forgotten as we discussed the new types of aircraft coming off the production lines, and the worsening situation in Europe.

In the Middle East the day started early, before the sun got too hot. As we walked down to Flights in the morning the sights and sounds were different from those in England. The character of light at six in the morning had an ethereal, unreal quality, as though seen through a veil. The colours, against the background of the all-pervading sand, were suffused with pink, the mop-heads of the palms standing out in an atmosphere clearer than the rose pink in which their trunks were bathed. The aircraft, in their sandy desert camouflage, looked foreign to us, though undoubtedly right for their purpose. Sounds were muted, and it was still cool.

When we'd handed over the aircraft our official duties were over, and those of us in blues could now change into our civilian lightweight kit. I bought a bolt of white silk in the local market, to be made up into shirts when I got home, and as I didn't want to pay import duty on it I took my parachute to the parachute section, pulled the ripcord, and got them to repack it again with my silk inside, making a mental note to remember to have it unpacked again when I got home: I didn't want to go hurtling to my death wrapped in shirting material if I had to bale out.

We travelled to Port Said and boarded the P & O *Narkunda* for the first stage of our journey. The Peninsular and Oriental Steamship Navigation Company had already invaded the language. As air conditioning did not exist in those days, in hot climates the forced-draught ventilation system merely blasted the already hot ambient air to make a furnace of the cabins. The coolest ones were those away from the sun – the port-side ones on the outward voyage and the starboard ones when coming home, so when experienced travellers were making their reservations they specified "Port outward, starboard home", shortened by the booking clerks to POSH. As travel was an expensive business in those days, the word posh became associated with the rich, so changed its application slightly.

Narkunda had come from Australia via Singapore, Bombay and Suez with the usual complement of passengers – rich Australians coming to have a look at the 'old country', tea and rubber planters, Indian Army and Air Force, and the Sudan Civil Service, all coming home on one of their infrequent home leaves. As officers, we travelled first class, and it wasn't as much fun as we had expected, as by our standards many of the passengers were on the old and stodgy side. Many had been forced by financial circumstances into the colonial life, as only there could they attain a standard of living comparable with their more fortunate peers at home. The social pecking order could be of depressing rigidity, and there was a pronounced lack of originality, both in thought and action. They lost their children early, when they were sent home to prep school in England, to live with aunts and grandparents for years at a time, and even to spend the school holidays with siblings at other boarding schools.

Due to the slaughter of their menfolk in the Great War there were now more women than men in England, and 'fishing fleets' of surplus young women made the voyage east to hunt for husbands under a tropical sun, the unsuccessful ones coming home as the cruelly-named 'returned empties.' Many of the wives lacked the mental resources to fill the too-empty days resulting from the absence of their children and the surfeit of servants. Many of the men would retire early through the ravages of life in a hot climate, to find impecunious retirement a bewildering affair, with no servants, the accelerated pace of life and the deterioration of manners. Some of the men drank more than was advisable. The British Empire was underpinned – upheld really – by a great deal of hidden human suffering and sacrifice.

We found it to be more fun in the tourist class, and had the best of both worlds, first-class passengers being allowed down into the tourist decks, but not vice-versa. However, the odd shilling to the deck stewards ensured a steady stream of selected popsies up the forbidden companionways, and we got many an envious glance from colonels' daughters imprisoned with their parents the other side of the lounge, and an equal number of disapproving ones from those parents because of the row we were kicking up.

We lazed the days away until we docked at Marseille, where we left *Narkunda* for the Paris–Dover train, and so on to Victoria, where the twelve members of No. 10 Blenheim Delivery Flight dispersed to their various units. I took the *Flying Scotsman* northwards, and arrived back at 233 Squadron on 5 June, flat broke but happy.

About a week later there was a distinct boost to my morale. While still the youngest pilot in the squadron, I had now been promoted to flying officer, had clocked up 600 hours, and had flown more types of aircraft than any other junior officer due to my habit of scrounging whenever I came across an aircraft that wasn't in my log-book. Two new boys had been posted to the squadron from their flying training school and I was given the task of giving them dual instruction to convert them to Ansons. I was starting to acquire status.

With the international situation degenerating at an ever-increasing rate, the ferrying of Blenheims to the Middle East was accelerated by training no more new crews: those who had been before would go again. Surprisingly, this wasn't popular, as most of us had shot our financial bolts on the first trip. But my name came out of the hat, and off I had to go to Thorney Island. An urgent call to Cox and Kings produced only forty of the fifty pounds I thought I would need for the complete enjoyment of the trip, and when you consider that a new Ford 8 cost only £100, you'll appreciate just what sacrifices a junior officer of those days had to make to ferry the King's aircraft out to Egypt.

No. 18 BDF was commanded by Sqn Ldr Buxton, who called

for our log-books:

'Edwards, I see you got to Ismailia in two days last time: that must have called for damned good navigation. And you had one Exceptional and one Above Average assessment at Tern Hill – you will be my navigator.'

I toyed with the idea of telling him of my previous navigation cock-up, but couldn't pull that one twice. I saluted unhappily and left the office.

But Buxton had two good ideas, one of them being that we would take three days over the trip, and the other that as the Middle East people had been so unstinting in their hospitality to previous flights we'd take a firkin of English bitter beer out for them, the five officers of the flight – with Cox and Kings' help in my case – chipping in for it.

The precious firkin was lodged between the spars of my lead aircraft, and No. 18 BDF slipped into the air on 26 July. The *Armée de l'Air* in Marseille were as hospitable as we'd been led to believe, and the next morning we made Malta, where the beer was put into the cold-room for the night. At Mersah Matruh the next day it was rushed into the hotel cellar while we refuelled, then back to our aircraft before we flew on to Heliopolis, our destination.

The beer was given two days to settle before being brought out, and I have a hazy recollection of an elderly flight lieutenant, 30 if he was a day, appearing at about two in the morning, and bellowing that as far as he was concerned they could chuck every Blenheim ever built into the Suez Canal if he had to put up with this sort of thing every time a bunch of clowns flew in a few more of them.

Within the week we had boarded the *Rawalpindi*, the next P & O boat to Marseille, where even the ship's newspaper mentioned the mounting international tension. But next day, lying in a comfortable deck-chair on deck, I really wasn't in the mood for that sort of thing. I ordered another gin sling from the deck steward, and reflected that there were worse ways of making a living than that offered to a junior RAF officer.

Bertie Mossford of 269 Squadron dropped into the chair alongside me.

'Bit of a bugger, this Polish business, isn't it?'

'I'm not really thinking, Bertie. Life's far too pleasant here.'

'Yes, but Austria's gone, Czechoslovakia's gone, and now it looks as though Poland's due for the chop. We've given Poland some sort of guarantee, you know.'

Reluctantly, I returned to reality. Bertie was quite right, of course: it really did look ominous, and I knew that my own squadron couldn't adequately cover our patch of the North Sea. We couldn't even *reach* Norway. We'd have to turn back sixty miles short of their coast, and any amount of German shipping could slip through that net.

And neither of us had any idea that in less than four months' time the flaming hulk of this big ship would slide for ever into the cold depths of the ocean as she went into forlorn action against the battle-cruiser *Scharnhorst*. Or that *Narkunda*, on which I'd made my previous return voyage, would be bombed to the bottom off Casablanca.

As we didn't know, we didn't worry, and all too soon the voyage was ended. But whereas I had arrived home from No. 10 BDF only flat broke, I now knew that I was horribly overdrawn, with a lingering suspicion that when all my Egyptian cheques came home to roost my overdraft limit of £40 was going to be exceeded.

But all this was brushed aside, as Leuchars was seething with excitement – in a few weeks' time we were to re-equip with a new aircraft, an America machine called the Hudson. With three times the horsepower, twice the range, more than twice the gun power and four times the bomb load, we would be infinitely more effective as a maritime reconnaissance squadron. In the meantime, as Squadron Armament Officer, I had to get our Ansons on the top line, so I supervised the checking of every aircraft's bombing and gunnery equipment, and that the bomb and ammunition storage was in order. When that was done I took the fortnight's leave that was due to me and went home to North Wales, by rail this time, as no aircraft could leave the station.

Tudor, my eldest brother, had joined the Territorial Army,

and was full of his two-pounder anti-tank guns. *Two*-pounders, for God's sake! They'd bounce off the German armour, from what I'd heard. He was also giving signs that he might want to transfer to the Air Force. We gassed about the services until Teddy, our other brother, chipped in. No militarist, though not a pacifist, he regarded us with a mixture of despair and amusement.

'You two really ought to stop playing toy soldiers', he said. 'There's one sure thing, nobody's going to get *me* into a uniform, Hitler or no Hitler.'

Whatever plans we had, events overtook us. Tudor *did* transfer to the Air Force, to die in his Blenheim at Rotterdam, and Teddy *did* wear a uniform, surviving the Western Desert and Italy, only to die in his tank in Normandy after D-Day. It was a good thing that we couldn't see into the future that late August day in 1939.

A telegram arrived, recalling me to my unit. I arrived back to find that we were officially mobilised for war. Surprisingly, my suggestion that I bomb-up our Ansons and get our machine-guns loaded was turned down.

'You can't have a bunch of aircraft with fused bombs and loaded guns in a hangar', said the Station Adjutant.

'But they'll be dispersed all over the aerodrome: it'll be quite safe.'

'Now calm down. We're not at war yet.'

'We damn well are, for all practical purposes.'

'Forget it. Anyway, if you did arm-up, what on earth would you do with all that explosive when Hitler climbs down?'

'We can defuse the damned stuff.'

'Look, it's a perfectly plain order – no arming-up. Now do be a good chap and bugger off. I've got work to do.'

I gave up and went back to the mess, where two letters awaited me. The more personal one was from an Australian millionaire whom I'd flown illegally some months before – it was an invitation to a week's deer stalking on his estate, that wonderful tract of Perthshire that I'd flown him round. It would have been a great experience, but I would have to refuse as we were all confined to the station.

I recognised the envelope of the other one. From Cox and Kings, it read, 'Dear Mr Edwards, We note with regret that the £40 overdraft which we granted to assist you in your second tour of duty in the Middle East has been exceeded, and now stands at £49 18s 4d. We trust that you will take immediate steps to reduce this to the agreed level.'

'Well, honestly,' I thought, 'not a single one of my aircraft armed-up, and fifty pounds overdrawn at the bank! What a hell of a way to start a war!'

Chapter Three

The Shooting Starts

No. 224 Squadron had already converted onto Hudsons, incurring a number of fatal accidents due to rushed training. And although they started their patrols to Norway *before* war was declared, they were already too late in their main object – the pocket battleships *Graf Spee* and *Deutschland* had already slipped out into the Atlantic in mid-August.

In 233 our conversion onto Hudsons was equally rapid, and after the docile Anson the Hudson was quite a handful, and just as 224 had had accidents through mishandling, so did we, though my particular contribution was due to misfortune rather than mishandling. With Sgt Hallam as navigator, I was one of six aircraft on an early-morning patrol; we were to get to the Norwegian coast by daybreak and do a line-abreast sweep of the North Sea as we turned for home in daylight. But it had been a misty night with a hard frost, and while the other five aircraft had been parked in the lee of some trees, mine was out in the open, and was entirely covered in a thick coat of hoar frost, which would not only increase the drag and slow it down but, more importantly, could affect the airflow over the wing and seriously reduce its lifting capacity.

'I'm not taking this aircraft', I told the crew chief. 'I'll take a reserve.'

'There isn't one, sir. All the others are on convoy duty at first light.'

So I was stuck with it.

'Then put some men on top of the wings with yard brushes, and get them to sweep the frost off the first few feet of the leading edge. (This was the area of the wing that was critical for lift.) And hurry, Chiefy.'

By the time this had been organised, the other five aircraft were following the leader round the perimeter track, so I was going to be very late, which would leave a ten-mile gap in the search pattern, but my machine certainly wouldn't fly in its present state. As I hassled the men with their brushes, the five aircraft took off and vanished into the darkness, bound for Norway. With hindsight, I should have let the men spend more time with their brushes, but that gap worried me, so I got the men off the wings, hustled the crew aboard and shot out on to the taxi track. I didn't strap myself in – I'd do that later. Sgt Hallam rode shotgun on my cockpit checks as we scooted round the perimeter and rolled onto the runway at full throttle.

With my unwanted fur coat of frost I had expected the speed to take longer than usual to build up, but not *this* long. The engines were giving their best, but despite all my efforts the tail would not rise enough. I managed to get off the deck in a fashion, but the Hudson was wallowing all over the place like a drunken duck. Then the line of runway lights which were my only guide ahead tilted, slid over to the right of the windscreen and vanished completely. As I flew into pitch darkness there was a thud and a rumbling vibration – the left wingtip had hit the ground. As I shoved on full right rudder and slammed the port engine into Emergency Boost, out of the corner of my eye I became aware that Sgt Hallam was leaving the cockpit for the relative safety of the cabin, and I didn't blame him one little bit: there was nothing he could do to help.

After that it was difficult to say which registered first – the violent impact, the shriek of tearing metal, or the enormous orange fireball as the 260 gallons of petrol in the port wing went up.

The rest was silence ...

It was dark, and very cold, though the sensation of undulation was pleasant – until interrupted by an irate voice, Sgt Hallam's I thought, though in view of the language it couldn't possibly be.

'Come on, you clot, we've got to get out of this.'

I preferred to revel in the delightful wavy motion, which

fitted the *Barcarolle* from *The Tales of Hoffman* to perfection. He'd got something, had old Offenbach – Tum-tee-tum, and riiise and fall, and uuundulate together …

The movements ceased to be soothing – became violent – and as my head made painful contact with something hard I enquired of the invisible world around me what the hell was up?

'We're jammed under the wireless op's seat, and you're on top of me. Until you get off me neither of us can get out.'

'If we're under the wireless op's seat,' I reasoned, 'where is *he*?'

'How the hell should *I* know? Probably mixing it with the gunner back in the turret. Now will you, for Christ's sake, get off me?'

'Sir', he added belatedly.

About time, too! (I'd deal with the insubordination later.) I extricated myself and gave Hallam a hand out. The floor of the aircraft was on a slope, and in the darkness the dim forms of wireless op and gunner made themselves known to me.

'Where the dickens are we?' I asked.

'In the estuary, sir', said the gunner. 'The back of the cabin's under water. We'll have to wade ashore.'

We stumbled down the sloping floor, pushed open the door, and slid carefully into thigh-deep water. But as we turned towards the tail and waded along the side of the fuselage it got deeper and deeper, and the mud muddier. Then night was banished into day as someone on the aerodrome fired a flare.

'The aerodrome's *behind* us', called the gunner. And sure enough, it was – we'd gone into the river *backwards*! We turned and waded back, climbed the steep bank to the aerodrome twenty feet above, and got into the ambulance …

My next memory was of being in Sick Quarters, with the MO giving me the once-over, and me apologising to the crew.

'Sorry, chaps', I muttered. 'God, Hallam, you do look a sight!'

'Taken a good look at yourself, recently?' asked Hallam.

I'd asked my batman to press my trousers the previous day, and had undone all his good work. They were torn, and mud from the knees down.

I went to my quarters and climbed into bed ...

There was to be a Court of Enquiry into the accident, and as Hallam and I worked on our statement the story unravelled. As my out-of-control Hudson flew into the darkness we were all set to dive head-first into the estuary at almost the exact point where, three weeks earlier, two good friends had crashed and died in a situation vaguely comparable. But there was an Anson parked on the perimeter, and our left wing ploughed into it, reducing it to matchwood. The Anson got its own back by tearing off our port wing, the ruptured fuel tanks releasing 260 gallons of petrol to be ignited by the exhaust flame. The impact swung us round like a Catherine wheel, to go backwards into the river, which, as I wasn't strapped in, was a life-saver. And once in the river the water put the fire out.

It was a brilliant solution to all my problems. I defy anyone to have done better.

But amnesia is a strange business. Twenty minutes must have elapsed between my climbing into the ambulance and coming-to in Sick Quarters, talking and behaving apparently normally as far as the rest of the world was concerned. I often wonder what else happened in those lost twenty minutes.

My 21st birthday was a large non-event. Bill Tacon, my second pilot, was doing the flying and the weather was lousy – 10/10ths low cloud and about half a mile visibility. It became pointless to carry on, as even if we'd seen a ship of interest we wouldn't have been able to find it again by the time we had come round in full circle. We turned back.

As a precaution against the time when I might conceivably have to ditch in the sea I had scrounged some ration rum – much stronger than the pub stuff – from a chap in the Navy. At about the time of day when I'd been born I produced my hip flask and offered it to Bill. 'My 21st birthday, Bill. Have a swig.'

'No thanks, I don't drink.'

This was quite true. Bill wasn't violently teetotal or anything – just didn't drink.

'Special occasion, you know.'

'No thanks.'

I toasted myself with a swig of the belly-warming stuff.

'This course you've given me,' Bill continued. 'The wind's backing. You *sure* it's OK?'

'Some coming of age!' I thought to myself. 'Big deal!'

In November the *Luftwaffe* started bombing our trawlers in the North Sea, causing great indignation throughout the country. We claimed that the trawlermen were non-combatant civilians, but the Germans said that maybe they were, but they could also be reporting their shipping and aircraft movements, which was a distinct possibility. They were also, of course, bringing vital food supplies into Britain, and as such were as much a legitimate target in total warfare as were the merchant ships that were getting such a dreadful pounding in the North Atlantic. But the emotional side of the affair was well played on by our propaganda people, and we all ignored what we did not want to know, and joined in the genuine feeling of horror at the bombing and machine-gunning of small, unarmed ships. Some day, I vowed, I'd get my own back on the *Luftwaffe*.

And that day came at the end of November 1939. I'd gone down to check on a Norwegian ship called the *Bruse*, and was climbing back to patrol height when the Hudson came alive to the gunner's cry of 'Dornier 18K ahead. Red oh-four-five. Low on the water.' I gave my front guns a test squirt and swept down on it, but the flying-boat was *on* the water, not flying. Withholding my fire, I returned for another look. Neither of the gun positions was manned, and the four crew were standing on the top decking. Careful examination showed that she was settling by the stern.

The North Sea in winter is a cold, comfortless place, so we went back to the *Bruse* and talked to her on the Aldis lamp. They understood our message, turned aside, and picked up the crew, after which we did some target practice with our machine-guns to accelerate the Dornier's sinking, while keeping enough ammunition in reserve in case we met with anything else on the patrol.

On our return we reported to the Ops Room, where the Station Commander said, 'You got the crew picked up? What on earth for? Why didn't you drop a bomb on them and blow them all to bits?'

'Sir,' I cried in horror, 'you can't do a thing like that!'

'Yes you bloody well can.'

'Hardly cricket, sir.'

'In case you've forgotten, Dopey, it isn't cricket we're playing. It's war. What price your trawlers now?'

Bill and I left the Ops Room in a confused state of mind. 'I'll bet he wouldn't *really* bomb chaps on the water', said Bill.

'Yet he's got a point, Bill. That bunch could find a way out of their internment in Norway (how right I was to be) and when they get back to the *Luftwaffe* they'll be shadowing our ships and homing in on the bombers again.' (The pilot could even have been the chap who would shoot down my eldest brother at Rotterdam later in the war.)

We walked in silent thought towards the mess, where tea would soon be on. I broke the silence. 'Look, Bill, life isn't all cricket and cucumber sandwiches, you know. We must take tougher action in future.'

'Agreed', said Bill; though somewhat unconvincingly, I felt. 'You know, I've never had a cucumber sandwich.'

That's the worst of being a New Zealander, I felt. Probably never even been to a vicarage tea party.

Quite the most pleasant job that winter involved the picking-up of survivors from a torpedoed merchant ship. In the middle of a huge oil slick were a couple of small life rafts with six or seven survivors on board. They looked a very cold, wet and miserable bunch, tossing away in the oil-sodden sea, surrounded by floating bits of wood, paint tins, buckets and cordage – all that was left of their world, now lying at the bottom of that icy sea. We dropped a smoke float to mark their position, went back to a destroyer that we'd recently passed, talked to them on the signal lamp, and within the hour had the satisfaction of seeing the men clamber up its side to warmth and relative safety. It isn't very often in war that you can do something constructive.

A few weeks later the German supply ship *Altmark*, reputedly with some of our merchant-seaman on board, taken prisoners of war by German raiders in the South Atlantic, was found off Bergen on a course back to Germany. A very strange international situation arose, as she put into a Norwegian port, where, in answer to our diplomatic questions, the authorities stated that they had searched the ship, found it to be unarmed, and that there were no British prisoners on board. We didn't believe them, or any other of their diplomatic telegrams that flew to and fro, and eventually took the matter into our own hands. The destroyer *Cossack* sailed into Norwegian territorial waters and boarded the ship in a style reminiscent of the fictional Captain Horatio Hornblower RN, releasing 299 prisoners without loss of life on either side. In those early days of the war, when almost every week a new setback afflicted our ill-prepared nation, it was a great boost to morale.

It had been bad luck for some people, but good luck for us – a neutral ship was torpedoed in shallow water just off the Bell Rock lightship, and she'd been laden with tins of butter and ham, presumably destined for America. As the tides broke her up, the coastal currents carried quite a bit of this desirable cargo onto the beaches of our bombing range at Tentsmuir. The discovery was made by an armourer of the range party, and as Squadron Armament Officer I was early in on the deal, acquiring a couple of tins of ham. Beachcombing became the station hobby, and with tins of butter also flowing into the station we now carried on our patrols sandwiches in which quarter-inch slices of ham squelched in a sea of butter. We openly pitied Bomber Command, flying their lumbering Whitleys on the asinine, but dangerous, leaflet raids over the Third Reich.

'I bet those poor buggers only have bully-beef sandwiches on those trips', opined Bill.

On 9 April 1940 we were nearing the Norwegian coast when one of the four retaining bolts of the emergency exit above my head became loose. I'd just made a note on my kneepad to tell the rigger about it after we landed when we sighted a Heinkel 115 floatplane flying north off the Norwegian coast. I called up the gunner. 'It'll probably be all front-gun work at first, Valentine, but get a shot off from the turret whenever you can.'

As we came up astern of the Heinkel his rear gunner opened fire, but at far too long a range in my estimation. When it came down to a more realistic 200 yards I pressed the gun button, and the twin Brownings clattered out their forty shots a second, cordite fumes leaking back into the cockpit.

I had the edge on the Heinkel, as I was astern of him. He twisted this way and that, but once the shooting started I was aware of little except the target and my gunsight, the Hudson being merely an extension of my mind as I operated the controls to keep the sight bearing. My tracers appeared as red dots floating up into the line of sight from the guns two feet below and arcing lazily towards the target, though not so lazily in reality – it took only a quarter of a second for them to get there. On the receiving end, the Heinkel's tracers appeared as spiralling smoke trails reaching out to destroy us: rather more threatening than the red dots I was firing off at him, I felt.

Our aircraft of the reconnaissance world were three times the weight of a fighter, 100 mph slower, and had only two guns firing forward, as opposed to a fighter's eight, so we were not the aces of combat who would be lauded a few months later in the Battle of Britain. I never, to my knowledge, shot down an enemy aircraft. Nor, on the other hand, did any of them shoot *me* down, and as the majority of aircraft which harassed us later were Messerschmitts armed with 20 mm cannon, and flown by full-time fighter pilots, they had far less excuse for such poor results.

I was getting home with *some* of my shots, as a plume of vaporised petrol came out of his port wing whenever he turned, and he was certainly connecting with *us*, each shot going through the cabin sounding like cracking a whip and breaking a glass window at the same time. The fight was taking place between two layers of stratus cloud a few thousand feet apart, and as he was heading for the upper one I went to full throttle after him. Almost simultaneously, the smoke trails of his return fire became more accurate, one in particular appearing to be coming right at me. There wasn't time to duck, and anyway it would have been pointless. There was a violent bang a foot above my head as a bullet hit the already-weakened emergency hatch, which flew overboard. The roar of the slipstream and the crackle of near-misses now became immediately apparent, and an immense draught flowed out through the roof, bringing every bit of dust, grit and grass seed from the cabin floor swirling round the cockpit. As I screwed up my eyes against the stinging grit I became aware that the controls were very stiff – as hard as iron. I opened my eyes for a split second and stole a look at the airspeed indicator, and wished I hadn't. Totally absorbed with my gunsight, I had failed to realise that the Hun wasn't climbing for the cloud layer above, but was diving for that below, and I had hideously exceeded our maximum permitted speed. I chopped the throttles and hauled out of the dive, but by the time I could see properly again the Heinkel had vanished.

It was fiendishly cold and noisy in the roofless cockpit as we continued our patrol, and I was very glad to make the Norwegian coast and turn for home. But April is not the best time for tanking along with your sunshine-roof open, and we were frozen to the marrow by the time we landed.

Eager to tell the world of our encounter, we burst into the Ops Room to find we had been well and truly beaten to the post. *Everyone*, it seemed, had had a combat with a Heinkel 115, and we joined a queue of 115-fighters eager to tell the Intelligence Officer their life stories. Everywhere, arms were raised and hands flew gracefully through the air, representing Hudsons attacking Heinkels, and Heinkels evading..

'What's up, Tubby?' I asked the chap ahead of me in the queue.

'Christ! Haven't you heard? Germany invaded Norway this morning.'

'Bit rough on the Norwegians, isn't it?'

It was *very* rough on the Norwegians, and was also going to be reasonably rough on *us* soon, though we didn't know it then.

The North Sea, which had gradually emptied of merchant vessels, now became busy with naval movements. The day after the scrap with the Heinkel I escorted one of our cruisers into the Pentland Firth, and the next day flew over Norwegian territory for the first time, hunting the fjords for enemy shipping. Later that day the battle-cruiser *Scharnhorst* and its attendant cruiser *Hipper* were sighted by another of our squadron, and all available aircraft were ordered to close and attack them, but we were too far to the south, and hadn't the fuel to reach them. Among the casualties in that attack on a ship virtually immune from damage from our 250-pounders was McLaren, the recently appointed commander of 'A' Flight.

As the Norwegian Expeditionary Force crossed the North Sea on the familiar too-little-and-too-late effort that was all we could manage in those early years of the war, the demand on us for escorts grew greatly, as did interference by the *Luftwaffe*. But it was not the slow reconnaissance aircraft we were now meeting, but their best fighters – the well-armed Messerschmitt 109s and 110s with all their advantage of the experience of the Spanish Civil War, and with the additional advantage that they stood a good chance of getting back to their bases if damaged in combat, whereas we had up to 450 miles of sea to cross before that option was open to us. And there was no Air-Sea Rescue service yet in our part of the North Sea.

From its Stavanger base the *Luftwaffe* harassed the Army and Navy units further north at Aandalsnes, and it was decided that the cruiser HMS *Suffolk* would bombard the aerodrome from the sea. (*Suffolk* was the subject of one of the ruder 'knock, knock' jokes of that time. She had been three years on the West Indies station before being brought back for a welcome Home Fleet commission, but no sooner had she returned than trouble blew up in the Far East, and she was sent off to the China Station, a highly unpopular move with the crew, who were just getting to know their families again. On her way to Gibraltar she passed a homeward-bound destroyer. 'Knock, knock', signalled *Suffolk*. 'Who's there?' obediently responded the destroyer. '*Suffolk*. ' '*Suffolk* who?' '*Suffolking* long way to China.')

The day before the bombardment there was a long planning session in the Ops Room, with the Navy well represented. It was expected that the Germans would react vigorously, so four aircraft would be laid on to spot for the gunfire – two Hudsons and two Walruses – or *Walri*, as we called more than one. *Suffolk* would catapult off a Walrus to spot for the shoot, and if there was any difficulty – 'Like when the poor sod is shot down', muttered Bill Tacon under his breath – the second Walrus would take over. And if *that* had any 'difficulty' I would take over, with Laurie Ewing, a New Zealander like Bill, taking over if *we* copped it.

'This is going to be a turkey shoot', continued Bill, rubbing it in unnecessarily, I felt. 'That coastline's going to be knee-deep in second-hand Hudsons and Walri.'

But there was a crumb of comfort.

'We're trying to get a Fighter Blenheim across from Wick to help you out', said the Ops Room Controller. Its five front guns would be a great help, but could a Blenheim *really* get to Norway with enough fuel to hang around and look after us?

We were to drop ten incendiary bombs in salvo on some likely spot on the aerodrome to try to start a fire, which would help *Suffolk* as an aiming mark, and follow it up with a flare over the centre of the aerodrome for good measure. Both Hudsons would carry a naval officer to spot for the gunfire, and a naval telegraphist to operate the wireless while on the shoot. My six crew were easily carried by the Hudson, as the incendiary bombs were light 25-pounders.

On 17 April I took off at 01.15, and circled in the darkness with my navigation lights on, waiting for Laurie Ewing to join me. But even after hanging around for five minutes we could see no sign of him, and as strict wireless silence was imposed until the shoot started we set off without him. (We found our afterwards that he'd had to return to base with complete electrical failure.)

We switched off our navigation lights, made a good landfall at Stavanger, and after contacting *Suffolk* ran in at 3,000 feet, some ineffectual anti-aircraft hate coming up at us. I dropped our incendiaries and the flare, in whose light I felt very naked, then went a bit out to sea to take up my spotting line. The radio was now the responsibility of the Navy: I was just a taxi driver.

Four gouts of ruddy flame pierced the darkness as *Suffolk* fired a gun from each turret, but I couldn't see the result.

Anyway, I was keeping a lookout for the expected horde of Messerschmitt 109s that were expected to be up my jumper as soon as it got light enough.

The gunner came up on the intercom.

'Aircraft coming up astern. Looks like a Blenheim.'

So they'd kept their promise.

But curling fingers of tracer smoke were snaking ahead twenty feet below me. I slammed the throttles open and turned hard left as the gunner's belated call came against the background rattle of his guns.

'He's opened fire. Looks like a Junkers 88.'

A forgivable mistake. In the still-poor light before sunrise the silhouettes of both aircraft were very similar. And they *had* half-promised a Blenheim.

All thoughts of spotting vanished. I'd let him get on my tail, and as our aircraft were of roughly similar performance there would be little hope of shaking him off if he was a competent pilot, which he showed every indication of being. From start to finish he dictated the action. All I could do was look over my left shoulder and counter whatever his next move was going to be. I pulled all the G in the world as I twisted and turned, with Bill dashing up and down from the observation dome in the cabin to the cockpit with extra advice on evasive action. The poor naval officer was flung all over the place, and clung on as best he could.

Some minutes later, as I looked over my shoulder yet again, a well-aimed burst from my gunner seemed to go in the region of his port engine. Either that, or he might have used up all his ammunition, for he broke away to the south.

At last!

I could now have a go at him. But by the time I'd made my turn to follow he was already a fair distance away. I raised the sight to allow for the additional gravity drop and fired a long, long burst at him, during which I became conscious of a prolonged tapping on my right arm.

It was the Lieutenant-Commander. He was pointing backwards and mouthing something. It clicked! My job wasn't to shoot down enemy aircraft; it was spotting for gunfire.

During the prolonged scrap we had got about twenty miles south of Stavanger, so I did a one-eighty and flew obediently back, where *Suffolk* was still at it.

Shortly after we rejoined her the midships four-inch guns started firing.

'Odd,' I thought, 'not very effective after the eight-inch bricks that are *Suffolk's* main armament.'

It clicked. The four-inch were their anti-aircraft guns. I looked around to find the air dotted with the puffs of exploded anti-aircraft shells, and four more went off as I watched. We weren't the only ones bad at aircraft recognition that morning. Not for the first time in this campaign – or throughout the war for that matter – the Navy would shoot first and answer questions afterwards. You could hardly blame them, really. There were several hundred men on board that expensive vessel, and only half a dozen in my Hudson – better to be sure than sorry.

We fired off the current recognition signal, and they stopped shooting at us.

When *Suffolk* had fired off her last salvo she turned out to sea at full speed and we turned south-west for Leuchars, happy with a job well done in the circumstances. Which makes it difficult to write the following. In the interests of the accuracy of this book I contacted the Naval Historical Branch to get the web-footed angle on the operation. Their courteous reply informed me that:

(i) In the absence of German fighter aircraft at Stavanger – they'd all been moved further north, apparently – it had been decided to use the Walrus aircraft.

(ii) Suffolk had catapulted off both her Walri and, happily, they had both got home, one to Scapa Flow and the other to Aberdeen.

(iii) Wasn't it a pity that none of the three aircraft had managed to establish radio communication with the ship, which had had to conduct an unobserved shoot. (Which would have been wildly inaccurate, I imagine.)

If I'd known about (i) I would have been far happier stooging up and down like a fat goose expecting to be plucked by an expected horde of Messerschmitt 109s.

I was very glad to hear about (ii), but how those Walri amphibians carried enough fuel for the return trip I just don't know. Maybe they rowed the aircraft the last few miles.

No. (iii), on the other hand, was an absolute facer. Neither of the naval crew in our Hudson had mentioned any failure of communication to me, either in the air or at debriefing.

In chastened mood I wrote back to the NHB. Would they be kind enough to elaborate? They were, and I wished they hadn't, as the second letter was even worse. The mistakes, omissions, failure to impart known information, unfortunate or plain daft choices all made Operation Duck – we hadn't even known its codename, but I feel that Donald Duck must have had a hand in it – an expensive and frustrating affair. The biggest single error was the choice of a radio frequency that Coastal Command had already found to be unreliable at dusk and dawn, so had been discarded as a night frequency. And as complete wireless silence had to be observed before the shoot started *Suffolk* could not be contacted to change it. She read one spotting correction from her No. 1 Walrus, and one from us. She fired off her second Walrus at about the time we returned from our ding-dong with the Junkers 88, and it had to revert to visual signalling with an Aldis lamp.

And apparently the flak that was fired at us as we did our incendiary run-in was enough to prevent *Suffolk* from identifying our incendiary bombs and the flare. To them it appeared to be just one more bit of the Guy Fawkes performance you could expect when you fly over a chap's aerodrome at four in the morning and drop bombs on him.

But what was to prove very expensive was that *Suffolk* had been ordered to sweep northwards after the shoot, to intercept some German destroyers, so her captain very wisely withdrew thirty miles out to sea before turning north. But the fighter escort from Wick which the Fleet Air Arm laid on to protect her expected her to be closer inshore, so made no contact. During the day she was attacked by thirty-three bombers, and was seriously damaged as she made for home. The first friendly aircraft arrived at 14.15, and eventually the battle-cruisers *Renown* and *Repulse* arrived to escort the struggling ship. But it wasn't until the next day that she crawled into Scapa Flow, with her quarterdeck awash and her steering-gear so useless that she could only steer on her propellers. She was in such a state that the captain ran her ashore on the first suitable beach, to prevent her from sinking.

When one reads about this sort of thing one wonders how on earth the war was ever won. The simple answer is that the other side made similar mistakes, of course, and in the case of the Nazi dictatorship far worse inefficiencies were heaped from above by Hitler's personal interference in his military advisers' plans. Just think how he could have mopped up the entire British Expeditionary Force at Dunkirk had he not held his armies back!

But it was disappointing to find that I had played such a lead part in one of the cock-ups.

The Norwegian scenery could be breathtakingly beautiful at times, especially the sunrises, as the sun struck the snow-capped mountain tops at different angles, each with its topping of pink icing. If the Hun wasn't about, and you felt like a bit of light relief, you could get an extra sunrise by diving steeply as soon as the sun came up, so that it vanished behind the mountains again. And a few seconds after levelling out it rose again, and you got your little treat all over again, though with inevitable and delightful differences, because the angles of the sun's rays had altered that little bit, and the subtleties of the colours with it.

Three days after the Stavanger shoot we did a reconnaissance of Haugesund, as it was thought that German naval ships were now using the port. As the Intelligence Officer wanted real detail I decided to do a low run a couple of hundred yards from the shore, as ship recognition is much more reliable in silhouette. As I skated along fifty feet or so above the water, Bill got weaving with the hand-held camera. Soon, through the opened window, came the familiar crack-crack-crack of machine-gun fire.

'Can you spot that bloody gun?' I yelled at Bill.

'Busy with this camera. Keep her going like it is, I'm getting some good shots.'

'You'll be getting some shots up your jumper if you don't watch out', I muttered.

Quite suddenly, the gunfire became much more accurate, each bullet cracking past with a flat staccato wallop. That gunner had the deflection worked out to perfection, and shots were now going through the fuselage with their usual splintery crash. It was high time to give him best.

Just ahead, a large bridge arched over the hundred-yard strip of water separating the mainland from Risoy Island, the sloping ground of the mainland and the buildings on the island making of the strip of water a steep-sided gulley in which I could get away from that accursed gun. And the waterfront here kinked to the right, which would also be to my advantage. Once in that gulley I'd be safe.

'I'm going under the bridge, Bill', I yelled, and did a right–left shimmy to get through the clutter of fishing boats whose masts were making the approach and exit more difficult than I'd hoped. Out of the corner of my eye I could see that Bill was still winding away with the camera – he wasn't the sort of chap to let a trifle like flying under a bridge interfere with good reconnaissance shots.

The bridge rushed closer, and I got right down on the deck, the tips of the propellers only a few feet – I hoped – from the water. And then I saw three *somethings* hanging down from the arch.

They came into focus as three hefty-looking wire cables, each capable of tearing off a wing. It wasn't on: I didn't feel like a trip to the knacker's yard yet, so hauled back on the wheel, yelling, 'I'm going over the top, Bill.' And fervently hoped that I was.

As the nose of the Hudson rose in the climb it completely obscured the bridge, and I sweated out the seconds, hoping that a tearing impact would not come, and also aware of a clattering noise in the nose. Then the parapet flashed by a few feet below the port engine. We'd made it!

I eased out of the climb, turned steeply out to sea in case that gunner was still in business, then climbed sedately away, becoming aware of a furious-faced Bill struggling up the steps from the nose, still with the heavy camera in his hands. I gathered that the clattering noise I'd heard as we swept over the bridge had been Bill and the camera being rammed down the stairs by the 5 or 6 G that I'd pulled.

'Can't you, for Christ's sake, give me some warning before you pull a stunt like that?' bellowed the puce-coloured face. 'You nearly broke my bloody neck.'

'Bill, if I'd taken you under that bridge you really *would* have broken your bloody neck', I explained.

He looked slightly mollified, and we climbed away in silence.

I sniffed. 'Can you smell anything?' I asked him.

'Not particularly.' I think he was still in a bit of a huff. 'Oh! Like hot metal, you mean?'

'Like hot metal, Bill. Have a good hunt round with the crew.'

All the instruments read normal, but, just in case, I slid back the emergency panel in the floor to expose the engine fire extinguishers. Bill came back and reported they could find nothing amiss

Then smoke started coming through the cabin heating vents. I took a squint into the port engine cowling, where all seemed well, Bill doing the same on the other side.

'This is it!' he cried.'

I put in the autopilot and joined him at the window, to see the crank-case of the starboard engine a streaming mass of green oil. There was a bullet in that lot somewhere.

'I'll take her up to 3,000 feet and stick around over land. If we get on fire and can't control it we'll bale out and contact the Norwegian Resistance. Put Gilbert back in the turret, and tell him to keep a good lookout for Huns.'

The starboard oil pressure started to drop, and the temperature rose to a dangerous level.

'I don't want it to catch fire, Bill, I'm shutting the engine down. We'll get home OK on one.'

I opened up the port engine a couple of inches of boost, re-trimmed the flying controls and put the starboard propeller into coarse pitch to reduce drag. But I left the ignition on as I didn't want the plugs to oil up. We might need that engine if we were jumped by any *Luftwaffe* boys who'd had an early breakfast.

Within a few minutes the smell and smoke had vanished, and we set off home. With the good engine running well below full power it hauled us along at 110 knots, and I kept our bombs on board as there was no point in jettisoning them with the Hudson coping so well.

Three and a half hours later we landed, to find that the damage was slight – a bullet had sliced through an external oil pipe, which was easily replaced, and the riggers soon patched up the fuselage. The aircraft was serviceable next day, in fact, and that night we flew her to Frederikshavn in Denmark.

'Reconnaissance at *night*?' I queried of the briefing officer. 'We're not bats.'

'Full moon', he came back.

'But what on earth can anyone see at night, even by a full moon, that's of the slightest use to the war effort?'

'How about *Admiral Scheer* for starters?' (She was a 'Pocket Battleship'.)

'Oh, no', said Bill. Or it may have been some other four-letter word.

'We've lost track of *Scheer*. She's been working up in the Baltic recently and has vanished from our recce photos, so she may be on her way out. It's a long shot, but she might be in Frederikshavn. The information is wanted urgently enough to justify a night search.'

I was doing the navigating, and was a bit worried. 'That's a fair trip, about 1,000 miles there and back by the time we've messed about.'

The IO looked a bit embarrassed. 'Well, actually it's a little bit further, really, as we don't want you to fly over Denmark on the way out. We don't want them to have any warning of your approach, or she might slip through our fingers again. Go up the Skagerrak well away from land, turn south-west into the Kattegat and come in to Frederikshavn from the sea. It's a long haul, I'm afraid, but we're increasing your range by leaving three of your bombs behind. You'll carry only one 250-pounder semi-armour-piercing, just in case she's there. When you've done the recce, signal us the result immediately, and you can come home straight across Jutland.'

'You bet.'

We got away from Leuchars before dark, so that I could get some accurate drifts before nightfall. The moon eventually rose in a cloudless sky, and the North Sea became a very romantic place, the moon-track reflecting beautifully on the sea. My thoughts drifted …

The intercom came to life. 'You asleep down there, Dopey?'

'Just thinking, Bill. What do you want?'

'Time to the next course alteration.'

I twiddled a few knobs. 'In eight minutes, Bill, turn to port onto oh-six-three magnetic for about twenty minutes. Then we'll go east for a while before turning south-westerly for Frederikshavn. I'll keep you up to date.'

Forty minutes later we were running towards Frederikshavn at 500 feet, so I came up out of the nose, clicked on the intercom and addressed the crew.

'Frederikshavn in three minutes. With this moon we should easily distinguish between *Scheer* and any merchant ships. She's 12,000 tons, with straight-cut upperworks in two lumps. She's got six four-inch ack-ack guns which won't amount to anything at night, and eight three-pounders and ten machine-guns which might.

'How low do you want?' asked Bill.

'A hundred feet should clear us of any steeples, etc. Lower if you feel like it.'

'Over or under bridges?'

This chap had got bridges on the brain after the previous day's do at Haugesund.

As we ran across the harbour mouth I couldn't see anything remotely resembling a naval vessel.

An automatic gun opened up from the harbour wall, a 40 mm by the rate of the muzzle flashes, but there was no point in telling Bill about it as it looked as though the gunner couldn't hit the floor with his hat.

'One more run, Bill.'

Still nothing.

'And one for luck. As low as you like.'

Bill did a real daisy-clipper across the harbour mouth, and it was obvious that *Scheer* wasn't there.

We turned for home, and I signalled base: '*Scheer* definitely not in Frederikshavn.'

We went up to two thousand feet, and as we flew over Aalborg aerodrome I considered dropping our bomb into one of the hangars, but didn't know how the invasion of Denmark was progressing, and didn't want to kill any Danes. As we left the land I fixed our departure point, after which there was little else that I could do until we made a landfall, as there were no detectable white horses on the sea on which I could take a drift. It was the sort of moon that, four months later, the people of Britain would know as a 'Bomber's Moon' as the Dorniers and Heinkels swarmed over our land and set fire to our cities.

I thought back to our fathers' war – it was in this patch of sea that the Battle of Jutland was fought, the first and last action between the massive Dreadnought battleships of the early twentieth century. Superficially, it was inconclusive, but the German battle fleet never put to sea again until it sailed to incarceration – and scuttling – in Scapa Flow after the Armistice of 1918.

After another hour or so of soliloquy I went up the stairs *en route* to the wireless operator, passing Bill in the semi-darkness of his cockpit, the instrument bank in front of him a mass of luminous dials, the only sign of movement being the slow oscillation, clockwise or anti-clockwise, of the synchroscope as one or other of the engines gained or lost a few revolutions.

I stepped over the wing spar into the wireless cabin, and felt that the Dutch artist Petrus van Schendel, who'd been dead these seventy years or more, might well have wished to paint the scene that I looked at, with Corporal Purves's face softly illuminated in the orange glow of his operating lamp.

'Get me a bearing from Leuchars, would you, Corporal?'

Four days later I was No. 3 of a battle flight sent to provide air cover for three of our destroyers somewhere off Bergen. It was a barrel-scraping effort, as the leader and No. 2 were from 'C' Flight, with Bill and me from 'B' Flight as No. 3. Not for the first time, I never felt really at home in 'strange' company. From hours of chewing the cud in 'B' Flight office I knew how 'B' Flight people thought and acted, and I didn't like the way our flight developed when, quite close to the destroyers, we were jumped by two Messerschmitt 109s. Our leader turned westwards at full throttle to lead the fighters as far from their base as possible, and dived to sea level to prevent them from getting underneath our tails, where our own gunners could not get a shot at them. In this I couldn't fault him, but he kept going at full throttle the whole time, which was giving our engines a real hammering, and we at Nos 2 and 3 were having difficulty in holding formation. The 109s were a hundred miles an hour faster than we were, so could catch us, whatever speed we were doing. By throttling back a bit, the strain on the engines would have been greatly eased, and with six of them belting away at take-off boost I felt that, sooner or later, one of them would pack up, in which case that aircraft was a dead duck.

Our gunner fired back as often as he could, and then, after about twenty-five minutes, during which time I'd heard no bullet go through the aircraft, the 109s broke off, possibly out of ammunition, but possibly also worried about their fuel supply, as we'd taken them a fair distance from land. I wished them ill on their journey.

But we had used so much fuel in going flat out for so long that not only did we have to abandon the destroyers, we did not even have enough fuel to get home. We made for Lossiemouth, our nearest base, to refuel.

Lossie was a grass aerodrome, and we landed in a wide V about a hundred yards apart. I was on the right, and after we touched down I took a look at Derry Matson a hundred yards on my left, and was dismayed to see that he was swinging towards me, and it looked as though we were going to collide. I abandoned my grip on the wheel, pulled hard on the brake lever with both hands and trod on full right rudder, but it seemed to have little effect on Derry's apparently firm intention of ramming me. With the undercarriage shuddering and groaning, the Hudson skeetered harshly over the ground until, at last, we seemed to be slowing down faster than Derry, and he slid across me only twenty yards in front of my nose.

'It's a fine thing', said Bill as he loosened his grip on the bulkhead, 'to arrive home intact after a dusting from a couple of 109s only to get nearly clobbered by a pal doing a lousy landing. Now let's get some fuel, and we'll probably get home for lunch.'

I looked out of the window before taxiing in, and it seemed strange that the hangars, towards which I'd been landing, were nowhere to be seen. I also became aware that I was left wing low, and a glance out of the window revealed a flat port tyre. Feeling very guilty that it was obviously me who was swinging into Derry, and not him into me, I switched off the engines. Then I noticed that Derry was *right* wing low. *He* had a burst *right* tyre, and we'd both been doing an inward swing, neither of us having heard the tyres burst above the engine noise. We all piled out onto the grass, and Derry and I made peace with one another.

In the afternoon a 'B' Flight aircraft diverted on its way out to patrol, and dropped off a couple of spare wheels, and next morning we could both fly again. But this was the third time I'd been diverted to other aerodromes for the night, so I had assembled an overnight kit in a cheap compressed cardboard attaché-case about twelve inches by eight, and packed it with toilet gear, a bar of difficult-to-obtain chocolate and a Penguin book for passing the time in the more dreary locations. I looked like a caricature of a city gent as I boarded my aircraft with this awful little thing, but this was before the days of the *image*, so it didn't worry me much. And it was put to good use two days later when we were doing a search in particularly nasty weather, with ten-tenths low cloud, and drizzle which reduced the visibility to a miserably unsafe degree. We were radioed to divert to Lossiemouth again before the clag shut right down, and I managed to scrape over the sandhills of the Moray Firth and touch down safely.

It was to be some days before we got home again. We were order to proceed to Wick, at the northern tip of Scotland, but the weather was still unflyable next day, so it was to be May Day before we got there, to find the station packed with Hudsons and Beaufort torpedo-bombers, dragged in to lend a hand, as the Army in Norway was being pushed into the sea, and the Navy was stretched to hell trying to keep them supplied. The Hun now had every airfield in Norway, and had destroyed all eighteen Gladiator fighters that had flown off the aircraft carrier *Glorious* to operate, under appalling conditions, from the frozen surface of Lake Lesjaskog. There were now no British aircraft in Norway.

As soon as I landed I was nabbed by my Flight Commander to make up a battle flight of three to cover ships off Kristiansund, almost 500 miles away. The details of the trip have faded from my memory, but we flew for 7 hours 20 minutes, which did not leave much for bad weather or combat manoeuvres. The following day we did a similar trip escorting some cruisers and destroyers, again returning to Wick for the night. That second night at Wick was my first, and only, experience of the Northern Lights. I had left the mess to go to my quarters when I became aware of darting coloured lights in the sky to the north. From the low horizon sheets and waves of multi-coloured pastel lights flickered and flowed across the heavens. In the dead silence of that cold northern night it was quite eerie watching that mute and lovely display, and I walked further out onto the aerodrome to ensure that my silent world would not be disturbed. And then, quite suddenly, it was gone. I went to my quarters quietly and wonderingly.

On the third day we set off for home, after first searching the Skaggerak for a reported German convoy. We did not find it, and fortunately met no 109s, for which we had the greatest respect, as the attrition of our numbers when the occasional aircraft did not return from patrol was now becoming a matter of concern.

Though on one occasion I *did* ignore their menace. We were stooging northwards along the Norwegian coast when Bill came bounding up the stairs from the nose and, waving an arm dramatically to starboard, yelled, '109s. Six of them.'

I looked, and saw nothing. 'You're seeing things, old boy. Now just get on with the navigation.'

He went back to his hovel in the nose, but was back in five seconds.

'For Christ's sake,' he bellowed, 'Messerschmitts. Six of the bastards. ONE OH BLOODY NINES. *LOOK.*'

I saw nothing but the magnificent Norwegian landscape. 'Liver spots, old boy!'

But Bill got so agitated that I rang the gunner. 'Gilbert. Mr Tacon says he can see six 109s, about green oh-five-oh. Have a look, will you.'

'Six 109s it is, sir.'

I still couldn't see a thing, so took up the binoculars, and sure enough, there they were, streaming smoke from their exhausts as they closed the range. I turned on the taps, spun round and made cloud cover.

'Sorry, chaps', I apologised to the crew on the intercom when we were safely tucked up in the cloud. 'Won't occur again.'

I wasn't flying the next day, and had a long ponder. Short sighted at the age of 21! They'd ground me. I caught the bus to St Andrews, swore a civilian optician to secrecy, and two hours later had been fixed up with a compact pair of steel-rimmed glasses that would fit undetected in the top pocket of my tunic. I was navigating the next trip, and when we were safely airborne and away from ground observation I put on my specs and came up out of the nose to test Bill's reaction.

'What on earth are those things?'

'Mark 1 glasses. Anti-109s, etc.'

Bill approved.

'Just one thing, Bill. Don't tell anybody.'

'Will do. Sorry, won't do.'

I kept the glasses in my hideous little attaché-case as part of my standard flying-kit, and it was well over a year before the medicos caught up with me when, through circumstances within my control, they said, I ended up with the cap of a 20 mm cannon shell in my eye socket, and failed the vision test on my discharge from hospital.

A week or so later Germany invaded France and the Low Countries, bringing the 'Phoney War' – the 'Sitzkrieg' – to an end. The station buzzed with excitement, but we hadn't got time to get all the gen, as Lord Louis Mountbatten's destroyer, the flotilla leader *Kelly*, had been torpedoed by an E-boat off Jutland, and I was No. 2 of the battle flight sent off to protect her. We arrived to find her with a pronounced list to starboard and under tow by another destroyer, and with an escort of two light cruisers and some other destroyers. She was doing about 2 knots.

We weren't jumped by fighters, but as we circled the mini-fleet I certainly felt – and this was well before the days when knocking the Royal Family became fashionable – that to risk so many ships so near to dangerous enemy-occupied mainland was attributable solely to Mountbatten's royal connections. And others felt that way. In the event she did get home, to be finally sunk in 1941 by the *Luftwaffe* off Crete.

The start of the Battle of France certainly put the kybosh on any reinforcement of the Norwegian Campaign, and from now on we were on a losing wicket. Within three weeks Dunkirk had to be evacuated, and it and Norway were just the beginning of an apparently endless series of defeats inflicted on our under-manned and under-equipped forces. The public accepted the situation, and we weren't spat on in the streets for losing almost every battle we fought, and I can remember only one occasion when criticism seemed a bit harsh, and that was when I found myself the only RAF type in a carriage full of army officers who, from their conversation, had obviously been booted out of France via Dunkirk. Few of our aircraft were seen by the beleaguered Tommies pinned down on the beaches, and my fellow-travellers wanted to know where the RAF had been. It was almost in vain that I pointed out that the few aircraft we could spare would probably have been a few miles inland, where they could inflict more effective damage on the Hun, and that the German aircraft that appeared over the beaches were those which, alas, too easily, had already run the gauntlet of the lonely Hurricanes and Spitfires to the east.

Towards the end of May eight squadron aircraft were detached down to North Coates Fitties on the Lincolnshire coast, to swell the numbers of a Bomber Command attack on Hamburg docks.

Bill and I were not too impressed by the bomber briefing, as it seemed so formalised. In Coastal we operated alone or in small numbers, in daylight, and against a variety of targets about which information could be scanty, or hastily assembled, as the war at sea could change very rapidly, and to a large extent it was an individual's kind of war. This bomber briefing followed a formalised plan which seemed designed to frighten the life out of you – ack-ack guns here, balloon barrages there, recognition signals, flares, flak and radio frequencies, this, that and the other. The target was oil tanks in Hamburg, and the recommended bombing height was 12,000 feet, which was about 11,800 feet higher than we were used to.

After the briefing Bill and I lay out in the sunshine alongside our Hudson – painted on its underside in the attractive Coastal Command silvery blue, hardly the thing for night work. I knew that with our equipment there wasn't a hope of hitting those tanks from 12,000 feet, and in the back of my mind was the idea that as there'd be no barrage balloon cables in the middle of the river – an incorrect assumption, as it turned out: they had them moored to barges – we could go along the Elbe at 500 feet, where they wouldn't be expecting to find an aircraft at night, drop down on the target and clobber it from a couple of hundred feet, then back to the river and away. Trouble was – would Bill agree?

To my delight he did, and at 21.25 hours we got away from the flare-path and climbed away, but stopped at 2,000 feet for the sea crossing. As we approached the Elbe estuary the flak started up on the boys at 12,000 feet, but this was only of academic interest to us, and I dropped down to 500 feet on autopilot, from where we watched the mounting searchlight activity and shell bursts up top, carrying on our peaceful way up the river.

'You know, Bill,' I said, not without an element of smugness, as we watched half a dozen searchlights illuminating a Hudson like a moth, 'if those chaps were down here with us they'd be as right as rain ...'

As I spoke, night vanished in a blazing haze of light: a searchlight had got onto us. I was completely blinded, so I stuck my head below window level, whipped out the autopilot and twisted and turned, flying largely on instruments. More searchlights got onto us, and then the light flak started – light in calibre, that is, like 20 and 40 mm, but very heavy in volume. We were the only target they had, and the night became aglow with streaks of flame of all colours, and now coming from both banks of the river. As we fled from one concentration of guns to another, the next series of coloured balls would rise lazily from the ground and float towards us, suddenly increasing in speed and becoming streaks of light a yard long, accelerating with amazing suddenness, and occasionally going through us with the usual splintery crash. The hosepiping of the tracer was so menacing that I ordered Dutch Holland out of the turret: I felt that if he started shooting back they would just shoot up his traces and *really* clobber us. I jinked as I'd never jinked before – a steep climbing turn to about 600 feet followed by an equally steep diving turn. To allow for the lag in the altimeter I pulled out when it registered 200 feet, unless a screech from Bill indicated an earlier pull-out if we weren't to hit the water.

With depressing regularity, shots went through the fuselage, and one considerable explosion – probably a 20 mm – blew the top of the wireless set to pieces, bits of shrapnel wounding the wireless operator. But as we turned the next bend of the river we had a moment's peace – no guns were firing and only one searchlight was onto us, and it was from dead astern. No longer blinded, I lifted my gaze from the instrument panel to see that the searchlight beam was a large circle of light, in the centre of which the shadow of our Hudson was completely outlined, and even the suggestion of the exhaust flames.

It was a moment of considerable beauty.

But it was not to last for long, being blotted out with brutal suddenness as other searchlights got onto us and we were back into the routine of being hammered from both banks by multi-coloured streaks of light, some of which connected with the usual splintery crash. The river became narrower, and two guns, one on each bank, did a really good traverse on us. I gazed unhappily ahead at the death-laden streaks of light not very many yards in front of the nose, ready to react the moment they showed signs of coming closer. But they dipped obligingly down, and I spared the time to wonder at the patterns the tracer now made as it bounced and skidded off the rooftops to the right of us. At Altona we turned into the southern branch of the Elbe, and after three more miles of hammering we got to the target, where, unbelievably, things seemed even worse.

I opened the bomb-doors and ran over the target at 300 feet, awaiting Bill's call of 'Bombs Gone', but it didn't come. He came up the stairs, said he couldn't see the target for searchlights and that I'd have to do another run. A tracer appeared through the upper surface of the left wing, but not near the petrol tanks, thank God. I glared unhappily at Bill and came round to do it, and it wasn't all that easy, as I could only take quick peeps at the ground or I became blinded, but I was pretty confident that I was on line.

But yet again Bill couldn't see. And it was just as bad on the third run, during which another 20 mm hit us somewhere, so I packed it in and brought the bombs away.

You must remember that this was early days in the war. Area bombing – in other words, blasting every single thing that stood or moved – had not yet come into vogue. The Hun hadn't started to flatten our cities, and the complete barbarism of blitzing – in which we later joined – hadn't arisen.

A year later I'd have had no second thoughts about it: I would have pressed the 'Jettison' button on the second run if Bill hadn't dropped them, and to hell with where they hit. But just beyond the docks, and well marked on our target map, was a hospital. We were peacetime trained to try and hit a specific target, and our job was reconnaissance, in which we again aimed at accuracy. All our training was against loosing off a load of explosives haphazardly into a populated area.

I didn't return to the river: I'd seen enough of the Elbe to last me the rest of my life, which had every prospect of being a short one unless we could get away from this incessant gunfire.

I fled westwards into open country, where a marvellous peace descended on the moonlit night. I kept low, but there wasn't a gun or searchlight in sight. I had to pull up to avoid some power cables, and then, as though to confound my decision to go higher, a gun opened up on us and aircraft hangars swept by underneath. We were over an aerodrome! With the bomb doors opening we came round and gave them the two-fifties in the hangars, and I remember thinking that the resulting explosion wasn't what I'd expected from such a load.

We got shot at as we crossed the German coast, so I went up to 2,000 feet for the sea crossing; then the moon went down. We came in on the flare-path at North Coates and I did a gentle wheeler onto the grass. The first two gooseneck flares went by under the port wing. But the third one seemed to be tracking into the wing root, after which no more flares appeared, and in the darkness I became aware of a horrible swing to port, and of the undercarriage shuddering under some pretty brutal treatment. Despite full opposite brake and rudder we slewed round, jarring and banging to a harsh final judder, facing the way we'd come. We'd got a flat port tyre. Again.

We got out and stood in the cold, waiting to be collected. There was a heavy dew on the grass, so we'd skidded more easily than at Lossiemouth the month before, and more extensively, as the skid had fully developed by the time I'd cottoned on to it in the dark.

We debriefed in the Ops Room, and it was a flat sort of business. The Intelligence Officer found us a nuisance, as the attack didn't fit in with the sort of report he was used to. He marked the form, 'Target not attacked', and we caught a few hours' sleep in the cold and crummy beds that had been dragged together for the visiting team. After breakfast we walked across the aerodrome to our abandoned machine, to find it already jacked up for the wheel replacement.

'You've got to hand it to Flt Sgt Radlett,' said Bill, 'he's an insubordinate sod, but by God he gets things done.'

Radlett was 'B' Flight's servicing NCO, and he came to meet us as we approached. Never one to be impressed by junior officers, his adjectives were limited to two.

'That's a fine bloody mess you've made of my effing aircraft', he opened.

'Not me, Chiefy, it was those trigger-happy goons across the drink.'

'Yes, but if you'd done what the rest of the squadron did and flown at 12,000 feet instead of arsing round at 200 it would have looked more like an effing aircraft, and less like a bloody colander. How the hell am I going to get this thing serviceable this side of Christmas?'

'Sir', he added belatedly.

Bill stepped in. 'Look, Chiefy, will she fly?'

'There's a problem with the elevator.'

We went round to the tail, where a 20 mm had blown a hole about six inches in diameter in its top surface.

'That's no great problem.'

'Take a look inside.'

He shone a torch into the hole, and the reason for his concern was apparent: a shell splinter had clipped about a third of the metal out of one of the arms of the bell crank. Whatever load the metal was designed for, it now possessed only two-thirds of the capability to carry, and of the three basic control surfaces the elevator was the most important. If control of that was lost at low altitude we were in real trouble.

'How long to fit a new one?'

'Depends on how soon we can get the first aircraft away to Leuchars, get the effing spare and fly it back here. Two more days if we're lucky.'

I thought of the cold, crummy beds that had been scraped together for the visiting team and didn't feel like two more days at North Coates.

'That damage was done at Hamburg, and I've horsed the aircraft round a fair amount without dropping to bits. She'll fly.'

As we spoke an armourer sidled up to me. 'Could I have a word with you, sir?'

I followed him under the aircraft, and as I looked up into the bomb-bay I knew why I was there.

'Shit!' I said despondently.

Hanging from one of the bomb-racks was the fusing link of a two-fifty-pounder. But only one!

There should have been four.

'Three of the four fusing circuits have been shot through by gunfire, sir.'

God! All that way for a single bomb, and that not on the main target. I hoped the Germans would have as much difficulty digging them out as we'd had delivering them.

Bill did the flying on the way home, and the navigation was simple on a coast crawl. Between reading snippets of news in the *Daily Mirror* and ticking off the estuaries as we flew northwards, my mind wandered onto other things. The cockpits were ideal places for philosophising when the heat was off, but I was becoming aware that the trend was increasingly away from the lofty, and was becoming more concerned with the practical matter of survival.

We'd been lucky to get away with the previous night's effort. And at increasingly short intervals machines were failing to return from patrol. The casualties were normally of single aircraft at a time, but one day a flight of three just vanished into the blue. Although I missed the old faces that would appear no more, I found that the new faces which replaced them caused me as much trouble, as I never quite seemed to catch up with getting to know them all. I was shrinking into a smaller circle of companionship.

And, with hindsight, a twist of fate was that at a well-established station like Leuchars the good social life and home comforts extended by the local people were doing us a disservice, though we didn't realise it. The contrast between being shot at by the Hun and, a few hours later, sitting in a comfortable drawing-room eating cucumber sandwiches as your hosts discussed the church bazaar was too much of a mental shuttle.

And talking of sandwiches, I'd stopped eating the ones I took on patrol, giving them to my wireless operator, who wolfed them happily. For some time I'd been aware that an almost perpetual feeling of hunger was abolished with almost the first mouthful of food, to be replaced by an acid, burning feeling in my stomach, which developed into a leaden feeling, as though I had a cannon ball in my stomach.

And bad weather, though entirely without the 'glamour' of shot-and-shell, was a wearing business. When the clouds were low, and rain and sleet reduced the visibility to only hundreds of yards, we often became squeezed into a few hundred feet of

The author's first flight was in this rotary-engined Avro 504 barnstormer, flying out of a farmer's field in South Wales in 1926. It carried his father, his two brothers and himself, as well as the pilot – quite a load for its 130 hp Clerget engine.

Trainee pilots at Brooklands Aviation's flying school, Sywell, Northampton, in October 1936. The author is back row, third from right.

Hawker Hart, a very charismatic machine. (A *Flight* photo)

A second-hand trainer after a pupil's attempt at a 'blind' take-off 'under the hood'. The directional gyroscopes which fed information to the blind-flying instruments were air-driven from the slipstream and in order to get them working the aircraft had first to do a circuit. Unfortunately, the instructor forgot to do this, so the pupil's reaction to the hideously inaccurate information which he was receiving had this result.

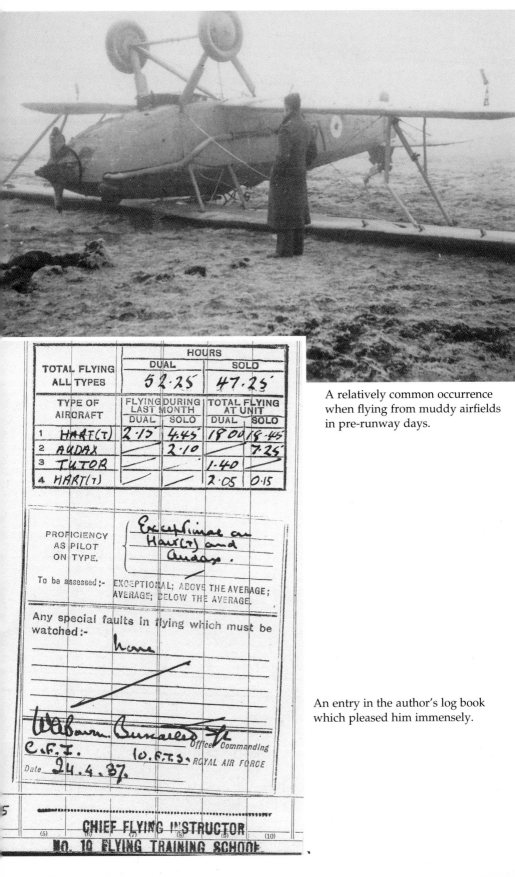

A relatively common occurrence when flying from muddy airfields in pre-runway days.

An entry in the author's log book which pleased him immensely.

An Avro Anson of No. 233 Maritime Reconnaissance Squadron.

The record-breaking No. 18 Blenheim Delivery Flight – UK to Egypt in thirty-three hours. The author is middle row, third from left.

ockheed Hudson, with which 233 Squadron was re-equipped at the outbreak of war. It was an normous technical advance on the Anson.

he author's first combat was with one of these Heinkel 115s, on the first day of the German vasion of Norway. Quite by chance his rear gunner shot out our cockpit roof, which meant a very ld trip home for us. (*I.W.M.*)

HMS *Kelley*, Lord Louis Mountbatten's flotilla leader, shown listing with her starboard rail under water, after being torpedoed by an E-Boat off Jutland. Note the crew had lined up on the port side in an attempt to minimise any further list. *Kelley* was towed home and repaired, being finally sunk off Crete in 1941. (*I.W.M.*)

A poor, but rare, photograph of a Messerschmitt 109 attacking me in the North Sea, 1940. We always went down to sea level when under attack so that the fighter could not get into the safety of our gunner's blind spot.

The bridge at Haugesund that I attempted to fly under in order to escape from a 'too-good' German machine gunner.

As the casualties mounted we were getting a bit twitchy.

I once had to do this at about 3.00am in the morning, and the sudden change of G as the relief valves snapped open – the elevator rapidly responding – woke the whole crew from their slumbers.

A Dornier 18K flying boat of the type we found shadowing the naval forces we were escorting. We ended up in a cloud shooting it out at about 20 yards range. (*I.W.M.*)

The bow gunner of a Dornier. A shadowy, sinister figure, but even more so in my case as the gun was pointing directly at my head. Rather daunting. (*I.W.M.*)

...)mm damage to the wing root. (*I.W.M.*)

...gunfire flat, which threw a great strain on the undercarriage and caused a big swing on landing, ...ften difficult to control. Other damage is also visible. (*I.W.M.*)

A rare mess party during a welcome period of bad weather. (*I.W.M.*)

Low-level attack on the blockade-runner *Nordmark*, sister-ship of the infamous *Altmark*, of earlier fame. The shadow of an attacking Hudson can be seen crossing the stern. (*I.W.M.*)

Scharnhorst, 26,000 tons of hell-on-earth. She had a seemingly unending supply of anti-aircraft guns. When we were returning from a fairly extensive search patrol we received a broadcast signal for all airborne aircraft to close and attack her. Our navigation check showed that we did not have enough fuel to reach her, even if we diverted to the Shetlands to refuel on the way home. Should one be ashamed to admit an element of relief. Our second-in-command, Squadron Leader Feeney, and Andy Wallace copped it in that attack. (*I.W.M.*)

On rest – my crew at an Army convalescent home. L to R: Sgt Gilbert (air gunner), Author, Bill Tacon (2nd pilot) and Tubby Davies (wireless operator) who, very obligingly, would eat my flying ration of sandwiches when, with my incipient ulcer, I could not face them.

Aircrew, No. 1 Flight, No. 2 School of Navigation, Cranage.

Wedding to Christine, 23 August 1941.

Burma – Stinson L5 artillery spotter, our main runabout for small airstrips. Over this sort of jungle terrain you hoped that your engine wouldn't quit on you.

With Bill Poynton, one of my armament staff. A few minutes later we narrowly escaped slaughter when a clown of an Engineer officer set off 2,000 lb of bombs only 100 yards away.

Rangoon – the author talking to Admiral Lord Louis Mountbatten, who gave us the sad projection that although we were winning the war, it was going to take another eighteen months to defeat the Japanese. (VE Day had long gone.) Then they dropped those wonderful atom bombs, and we all came home much sooner than expected.

During my travels, at Karachi I managed to scrounge a flight in the Mustang, the fastest thing I ever flew – getting 500 mph out of it. Then I realised that as a responsible married man soon to be demobbed I shouldn't push things too far, so throttled back.

Palam, Delhi, late 1945. In India I had a staff job that wasn't very interesting, but it entailed traveling the length and breadth of that fascinating country.

Home at last! With Christine, Guy and Susan.

airspace between the grey wispiness of the cloudbase and the heaving desolation of the North Sea. And if you once lost sight of the sea in a wisp of cloud you had to pull up immediately into the overcast, with no chance of letting down through it.

You climbed, hoping that the cloud would break up enough to give you a safe enough clearance above the belt of hills just inland of the coast to enable a safe landing back home.

I was quite glad when we got back to Leuchars, and the philosophising could stop.

At about this time our Hudsons' defences were improved to take a Lewis gun firing sideways. A window on each side of the cabin was made detachable, and a gun mounting fixed outside. When required, the window was pulled out and the gun slid into its socket. If we were attacked from the other side the gun was heaved out and stuck out of *that* window. With its 97-round ammunition drum it was quite a thing to lug around the cabin, and I well remember Bill Tacon's displeasure one day when he was doing the flying. The gunner came up: 'Four 109s two miles astern. Flying south.'

'Let me know if they alter course.'

We were already out to sea, so maybe they hadn't seen us yet. I stuck the Lewis out of the starboard window as Bill dived for the deck, where the strong wind that was giving us a lot of turbulence had churned the surface into a mass of white horses, the best camouflage there was.

We waited anxiously for the gunner's next call, which was a welcome 'They've passed astern. Still flying south.'

We gave them a few more minutes while Bill came up to cruising height again, and I lugged the heavy Lewis inboard just as we hit another patch of turbulence. As the muzzle of the out-of-control gun hit the cabin floor I inevitably pressed the trigger, the internal blast and noise being considerable. But I missed my foot. God knows what epithet the squadron would have appended to 'Dopey' if I *had* shot myself in the foot. There was a blast hole in the floor, and we took up the floor panels to peer into the bomb-bay, seeing a hole in one of the bomb-doors. The bullet was now safely at the bottom of the North Sea.

'Any more funny tricks up your sleeve?' glared Bill as I passed him and went down into the nose.

'You damn nearly deafened me.'

'Scared you a bit, too, I'll bet', I said, somewhat cruelly.

'That, too', said Bill.

A week later, at five in the morning, three crews assembled in the Ops Room, and they weren't happy: the haar of the east coast had settled in – low cloud, bad visibility, a raw sea mist that bit into one's bones. It was the sort of weather where you'd probably have to land at the first aerodrome that was clear.

Derry Matson was flying the third aircraft. 'Derry, do me a favour, will you?' I asked.

'Certainly, Dopey, anything to oblige.'

'If we're diverted to Lossiemouth will you keep out of my hair, and not do a bloody great swing into me like you did the last time.'

'Pot calling the kettle black, would you think?'

The Controller was speaking. 'We're sorry to drag you out in such bad weather, but the Navy is stretched to hell, and we think the Hun is running a convoy north to Trondheim. If you have to divert on the way back you can use Montrose, Dyce or Lossiemouth.'

At 06.50 we took off into the clag, the cloudbase at 800 feet and the drizzle piling opaquely on the windscreen. Ahead, things were distinguishable only at about 400 yards, a distance we covered in five seconds. Subtract reaction time, and it didn't leave much time to avoid obstacles.

Sideways, as usual, we could see a bit further. But aircraft don't fly sideways.

Tension rose in the aircraft as we flew eastwards into a lowering cloudbase. Was there *any* point in carrying on with this patrol? How much sea were we covering in our search – a band half a mile across? If we came across some ships, five seconds later they would be lost astern of us. The best pilot in the world couldn't guarantee to hold a consistent Rate 2 turn in these conditions for exactly 360 degrees, and hope to come across those ships again. And I'd be more concerned with keeping my left wingtip from hitting the water.

Tubby Davies, my wireless operator, pushed a message into my hand: Sgt Muir, ten miles to the south of us, was abandoning the search and returning to base.

I was forced down to 300 feet in the murk, and the worst of flying into a depression was that as the barometric pressure dropped it also caused the altimeter to over-read. Three hundred feet on the clock could possibly mean that you were as little as 250 off the deck.

Tubby Davies put a second message into my hand: Derry Matson had packed it in, too.

I decided to give it a few more minutes. I fantasised …

'Daddy, you know the heroes of the Great War!'

'What, chaps like Albert Ball and Rhys Davies?'

'Yes. A friend of mine said they all died gloriously, facing fearful odds. Well, *you* died for your country, didn't you? Did *you* die facing fearful odds?'

'I certainly did.'

'Tell me *all* about it, Daddy. Don't leave out a thing.'

'I hit a bloody hill, son.'

Another message arrived, advising me to divert to Thornaby, which I just couldn't do: I hadn't even got the fuel to get to Montrose. It would have to be Dyce, Aberdeen, which I knew slightly. After another hour, never above 400 feet, we hit Peterhead and turned south. As Aberdeen harbour came up I turned sharp right, roaring over the city at 200 feet. I throttled back to 110 knots, and put the undercarriage down. The aerodrome boundary appeared, though I couldn't see the far one. I knocked the flap lever down to 100%, and landed downwind. The hangars emerged from the murk, and I came to a stop a couple of hundred yards short of them, seven hours to the minute after we'd taken off. It had been a very long seven hours indeed.

Bill was on leave, so I did the next trip – a reconnaissance of Bergen harbour – with one of the new boys. The briefing was odd – 'You may attack a merchant ship only if it attacks you', said the Controller, or something like it. I pointed out that I'd never had a merchant ship take off from the sea and try to do me in.

'You know perfectly well what I mean, Edwards, don't live up to your name. All right, I'll explain. Most, though not all, Norwegian merchant ships have been impressed into German service, so if one opens fire on you then you can reply. But don't start blowing Norwegians to Kingdom Come unnecessarily.'

With Roy navigating, we ran low into Bergen harbour, packed with so much shipping that we couldn't single out any individual ship for attack. Then tracer arose from one of them, too close for comfort, but there was no hope of bombing it without damaging many others. I felt enraged at the ease with which he could fire at me with apparent impunity. I stuffed the nose down and pressed the gun button, and we swapped gunfire as the range closed. Then I thought how darned stupid an action it was. He could possibly shoot me down, whereas I couldn't do any real damage to a steel ship with machine-gun fire. I pulled out and fled from the harbour at 500 feet.

Then some oil storage tanks appeared. They'd do. We dropped our four 250-pounders, the nearest being fairly close, but not, alas, near enough to damage them, and we flew into the peaceful country to the north of Bjornefjord.

Then maddeningly, after we had dropped our bombs, a ship of about 2,000 tons flying the Nazi flag appeared. I circled round, climbed so as to give me a longer dive, shoved the nose down and kept my finger on the gun button for the longest burst I'd ever fired. Shots hammered out of the Brownings, and I could see my tracers and incendiaries winking away on the steelwork of the bridge. Then there was an explosion and a pressure wave from up in the nose. Something had hit us there, and if they'd done it once they could do it again. I fled out to sea.

Mysteriously, we could find no damage there: no entry hole or other sign of damage, and we had to wait until we landed and the armourer arrived to unload and clean the guns. The right-hand gun had jammed because a round in the feed-way of the breech block had exploded. I had fired such a burst that the right-hand gun had got so hot that, in the twentieth of a second that it remained there before it was rammed into the breech it had cooked off. The gun must have been nearly white hot.

'I'll put new barrels into these guns, sir,' said the armourer, 'they won't be much use after this.'

It must have been about this time that the attention of all personnel was drawn to an Air Ministry circular advising regular servicemen to subscribe to a system called the National Insurance Scheme, or something like that. This, it appeared, would help if we were ever unemployed in the future, and it would cost about five shillings a week – more than £1 a month.

At the rate our casualties were mounting as the campaign dragged on there wasn't the slightest guarantee that I would survive to benefit from the system. It looked a complete waste of money, so I didn't subscribe.

It was a very unwise decision, as I would find out to my cost in a few years' time.

Chapter Four

Shoot-out in Cloud Nine

Things were going badly. In the space of a few weeks Denmark, Holland and Belgium had been overrun; the British Army was falling back in France, and we would soon evacuate Norway. The aircraft carrier *Glorious* had been sunk, and on the day that we *did* quit Norway Mussolini decided to bring Italy into the war on Hitler's side for some easy pickings.

And Bill and I collected our DFCs at Buckingham Palace.

A little later I found myself in command of 'B' Flight. Cooper, our Flight Commander, had gone off on some mysterious detachment from which he never returned to the squadron, and rumours circulated that he had been taken prisoner in North Africa somewhere. As the senior surviving officer I inherited 'B' Flight, but not, unfortunately, the acting rank and pay of a flight lieutenant, as Cooper was still officially a member of the squadron.

With ground fighting a thing of the past in Norway, the Germans now put more resources into the defence of ports and aerodromes, and the amount of flak being flung at us was increasing. To a large extent, this was reflected in the differing attitudes of pilot and navigator during medium-level bombing runs – 1,000 to 3,000 feet – despite the fact that we did both jobs, turn and turn about. The bomb aimer was a busy man. After putting the numerous settings into the bombsight – airspeed, height, barometric pressure, bomb terminal velocity, trail angle, wind speed and direction – and the enemy's speed and direction when bombing ships – he then had to guide the pilot towards the target, ensuring it moved down the bombsight drift wires, and trying to correct the pilot's inevitable small errors in speed, height-keeping and levels. Yes, the spiralling smoke trails of tracer coming up were disconcerting, but his sideways view was limited, so he did not see so much, such as the puffs of exploding heavy ack-ack to the side. He was busy, and if the pilot was twitchy that was *his* affair.

But the pilot saw everything, including those puffs. And despite having to concentrate on accurate flying he was not so mentally active. His conversational style tended to be of the 'How much longer before you drop those bloody bombs?' sort of thing, as opposed to the more soothing approach of the bomb aimer who, while getting across his regret that the pilot's training appeared to have been carried out on the Big Dipper at Blackpool, he was not to worry, and just carry out the eminently sensible instructions he was receiving. Eventually, of course, up came the welcome 'Bombs gone', and you both got the hell out of it.

I've often pondered on our habit of going in on these bombing runs at cruising speed. We would have been shot at for a shorter time if we'd gone in at maximum revs, but the only time I'd suggested such an intelligent approach to Bill he'd stamped on the idea, as he'd already made all the settings on his bombsight, and he wasn't going to frig about altering things. So in we went at cruising revs. Pavlov's dogs couldn't have done it better.

Part of our job was plotting new gun positions, an incentive to leave the area being provided by the very thing you were looking for. On one patrol, as we left Bergen harbour well below the level of the hills to keep below the radar, I had my side-window open, and was surprised to hear a machine-gun firing *down* on us from further up the hill. We gave him best and beat it. After that chap at Haugesund had plugged up one of my engines a few weeks earlier I had lost interest in trying to damage a hundred pounds' worth of machine-gun by putting a whole aircraft and crew at risk.

On Midsummer's Day I patrolled an eighty-mile stretch from Bergen to Karmo without seeing anything except a rapidly diving sub in a 'submarine sanctuary'. These were areas plotted on all our charts where our subs could resurface to charge their batteries without being attacked by 'friendly forces'. But Derry Matson, some miles to the north of us, had had an eventful time. He'd made an abortive attack on a German merchant ship, which failed because an electrical fault caused his bombs to drop off their racks the moment the bomb-doors opened, after which he was chased into cloud by Messerschmitt 109s. After hiding for a while he emerged from the cloud to find the 26,000-ton battle-cruiser *Scharnhorst* and her escorts sailing north. He sent an urgent signal to base, and all aircraft were ordered to close and attack. But by this time we were well on our way home, and perhaps I should be ashamed at an element of relief that swept over me when I checked her position and found that we had not got the fuel to reach her. She was 26,000 tons of hell-on-earth firepower, and would have the usual umbrella of protective fighters over her. We carried on home, and spared a thought for those less fortunate. In any case our attack would have been useless – we were carrying 250 lb general-purpose bombs which, in the low-level attack that was the only possibility in that weather, wouldn't have had anywhere near the speed to penetrate the armour, and the relatively light bomb casings of a GP would have shattered on hitting the plating. But our second-in-command, Sqn Ldr Feeney, and Andy Wallis *did* find her, and were shot down by the escorting fighters. When last seen, *Scharnhorst* was steaming north-east, and would be well out of our patrol area by the morning. But just in case she wasn't, I led a flight of three on a hunt for her. We got away from Leuchars at 05.45, and by 07.00 had come up with a couple of our cruisers, which asked us by signalling lamp if we could do an anti-submarine escort for them. We did this until 07.35, when they asked us to go to the assistance of a second force of four cruisers and a destroyer, which were being shadowed by a Dornier 18K flying-boat. The 18K had a very characteristic shape, with two engines in tandem – one behind the other – and was armed with a machine-gun in each of its two open cockpits – one in the bow and one amidships. I found the Dornier just below the clouds, and attacked with my front guns, but it climbed rapidly away into the overcast. In the hope that it would break cover on top and give me another chance at it, I followed into the cloud and ran an instrument check, to be fully prepared in case we *did* meet on top. But a few seconds later I had the shock of my life to see the Dornier only thirty yards ahead of me. In the fog of the cloud it looked black and enormous. In a one-in-a-billion chance I'd followed almost directly in his wake, though a bit off to one side. And at the same time that I saw him his midships gunner, in his open cockpit, saw *me*. A sinister-looking fellow in his black leathers and goggles, he looked like an executioner as he went for his gun ring and swung the gun towards me. This was no time for the niceties of gun-sighting. I thumbed the gun button and swung my Hudson directly at him. The red dots of my tracers hosepiped down his engines, striking sparks all over the place, and swept down towards him. To my intense relief I beat him to the draw. His gun cocked up into the air as he slumped down in his cockpit.

'Poor bugger!' flashed immediately through my mind, but it was all the time I could spare him, as my right wing got into the Dornier's slipstream, after which there was no more chance of hitting anything from my wallowing pig of a Hudson. I became conscious of the hundreds of rivets in his metal skin, of his rudder hinges and the old-fashioned gun mounting with its gun cocked drunkenly upwards, of the wireless aerials and a dozen other things.

But we were about to collide.

I hauled the right wing over his rudder and tailplane before my starboard propeller carved them to bits. While this would have knocked him out of the skies, it wouldn't have done *me* much good – the damaged propeller would have been completely unbalanced, and would probably have shaken the engine out of its mounting.

With no means of slowing down I continued to overtake, coming into the view of his front gunner, a repetition of the black menace I'd just dealt with. He was waiting for us to slide from behind the protection of his front propeller, as he couldn't fire yet without the risk of shooting it off. We gazed at one another through its diaphanous disc, his gun tracking remorselessly forwards, and always pointing at my head. I could not return his fire as my own guns would no longer bear, and my gunner would be unable to power his turret forward in time.

I lost my nerve, and kept ducking below widow level to shut out the sight of that awful black devil and his gun. A pointless exercise, as the bullets would come through the metal side of the aircraft just as easily as through the glass of the window.

As, like a hypnotised rabbit, I raised my head yet again, his gun muzzle flashed crimson, and twenty shots a second hit us. It sounded as though the Hudson was being destroyed about our ears.

But he shot a foot too high and stopped a yard too soon. That much lower and longer and he would have killed both pilots and the gunner, and probably the wireless op as well. Unable to reply, I'd had a bellyful, and had put the wheel hard over. We parted, never to meet again.

Most air action is impersonal, metal aircraft shooting at metal aircraft, but that bar-room brawl of a shootout with the Dornier was on an altogether different, and very personal, plane. I thought a lot about it on the way home. The front gunner had certainly damaged my aircraft, but I *would* get home. The chap in the waist cockpit, however, was another matter altogether. Like the rest of us, he would have had parents, brothers and sisters, perhaps a wife and children. It was him or me, but it would have been nice to think that maybe he'd just finished a banana before we came on the scene, and had slipped on the skin, or something. (I've never met anybody – even fighter pilots whose only job it was – who'd had such a close-up argy-bargy of this sort *in a cloud*. Or even in clear air for that matter. If the *Guinness Book* of *Records* had been invented then I'm sure I could have made it.)

Back in the Ops Room we learned that France had now finally surrendered. Despite the apparently hopeless position we were in – imprisoned in our island with inadequate arms – I remember a feeling of relief that at last we could run the show on our own. The whole war seemed simpler now, and it never occurred to me that logically we would probably lose it. What saved us, of course, was the English Channel. If we'd been part of the mainland of Europe we would have followed the rest of the Continent into bondage. With the unforgettable and inspiring leadership of Winston Churchill, his resonant voice growling defiance at the dictators in his broadcasts, the British people were knitted into the magnificent band of brothers that they became in 1940. The cynical will say that it was a common fear, and nothing else, which united us, but unite us it did, and only those who were old enough in 1940 to appreciate what was going on will know what it was like to live in an almost selfless society, proud of its country, and all working to a common end. It was a wonderful time to be British!

The next three weeks were remarkably peaceful. The day after the scrap with the Dornier we escorted a small naval force into Rosyth, probably the last elements of the many ships which had been scouring the North Sea for *Scharnhorst*, and as the Army had been kicked out of Norway most of our work settled down into routine U-boat/shipping sweeps of the North Sea between Scotland and Norway.

It was at about this time that all non-commissioned aircrew were given the rank of sergeant. NCO pilots had held this rank for years, but the wireless operators and air gunners held whatever rank they had achieved in their basic trades. The wireless operators were already plying theirs, of course, but the gunners were volunteers from the fitters, riggers, electricians and so on who trained in gunnery in addition to their normal jobs, for which they received the magnificent 'flying pay' of – I think – sixpence a day. The crewmen I flew with most often were Cpl Davies as wireless op, and LAC Gilbert as gunner, and the first time they appeared with three-bar chevrons on their sleeves they looked somewhat self-conscious, and perhaps a bit bewildered. Sergeants' messes since time immemorial had been peopled by old sweats from the Great War and the North-West Frontier of India. In their mid-forties, their blood thinned by tropical heat, they took a long time to adjust to the 19-year-olds who crept fearfully into their holy of holies that first day.

And *commissioned* air gunners were now appearing, one of the first being the unfortunate 'Dutch' Holland who had been with me on that pyrotechnic night raid on Hamburg. He swore he'd never been the same again, and he nearly wasn't. I had brought him out of the turret in case the Huns really clobbered us by shooting up his traces. So he was standing opposite the wireless set when the 20 mm blew it to pieces, bits of shrapnel flying across the cabin. He was unhurt, but you could almost see the outline of a man on the opposite wall, surrounded by pock-marked upholstery. Our wireless operator was wounded, though not too badly, in the arm.

Another happening during this quiet period was an organised mess party, which were few and far between, as we could be called on to fly at any time. For some reason, Bill and I had missed out on the publicity, and we landed from a patrol late at night to find that the party was to take place the next day, when we were scheduled for another evening trip. We didn't want to miss it, so swapped duties with an all-sergeant crew who were to take off at some god-awful hour of the morning. We would get only four hours' sleep. At the appointed hour I staggered into the air, set off for Norway and plugged in the autopilot. Time and again I nodded off, to jerk into wakefulness for a few seconds before falling asleep again. As my head jerked up yet once more I saw the surface of the sea flitting past in the light of the port engine's exhaust flame. We were about to hit!

I hauled back on the wheel with all my might, the hydraulics of the autopilot resisting until the relief valves suddenly snapped open, when my full backward pressure came suddenly on the elevator. We shot up in a G-laden climb, the sleeping aircraft waking immediately, and the intercom crackling into activity as the anxious crew wanted to know what on earth was going on. I realised that the surface of the 'sea' was, in fact the top of a layer of stratus cloud, and that we were still safely at 3,000 feet. Queries ranged from Bill's 'What the hell d'you think you're doing?' to more respectful – though suspicious – ones from the wireless op and gunner.

It was time to exert my authority, and it was unfortunate that I heard a voice bleating over the intercom, 'Sorry, chaps. Won't occur again. Must have fallen asleep or something.'

My apology was followed by silence. I imagine they'd all

fallen asleep again. In an effort to stay awake I slid back the side-window and stuck my head into the 140-knot slipstream. *Anything* to stay awake.

The slow lightening of the sky ahead signalled the approach of dawn, and the world became light enough for us to start our reconnaissance, and to be aware that just as we could now see, so could we be seen. The problem of sleeplessness vanished as we came up to the Norwegian coast, turned ten miles south, and set off for home. There was nothing to report, not a hostile thing in sight. We were soon clear of any likely danger, and I stayed awake long enough to get the Hudson on the deck in reasonable fashion. But all for nothing in my case.

Bill made the party, but by the time I got to bed I dropped into so deep a sleep that the party was over by the time I woke up.

Dutch Holland waxed lyrical about the females at the party, waving his hands sinuously in the air to reinforce the details he gave me about his particular bird. Sensing my disappointment, he started to console me.

'I know, I know', I broke in, and repeated those words of wisdom that Jocelyn du Boulay had spoken three years before, when that flock of sparrows had mucked up our Audax: 'Only sparrows can fuck and fly. But hasn't it struck you that I've been doing quite a lot of flying recently, and could do with a change?'

Our patrols continued over a quietening North Sea. But despite the obvious reduction in enemy activity in our theatre I still got that gut-tightening burning in my stomach as we approached the Norwegian coast in scanty cloud cover. Common sense said that many of the *Luftwaffe* fighter squadrons must had been withdrawn from Norway to back their offensive in the south, but still the occasional aircraft failed to return from patrol, the obvious cause being that they had fallen to Messerschmitts. Morbidly, as I flew eastwards on one patrol, I dwelt on my unhappy lot, but hoped that my inner resolution was not becoming obvious to others, particularly to my own crew, and especially to Bill. My standards were not physically slipping – they just required a larger effort to maintain.

Then the greyness of the horizon off to port had become greyer, more dense. As the cannon-ball in my stomach increased in weight I took up the binoculars, which confirmed the accuracy of its forecast.

Ships! And not ours, or we'd have them on the plot. I pressed the intercom.

'Captain to crew. Ships bearing red oh-four-oh, fifteen miles.' Bill came up the stairs and took over the binoculars as I turned towards them. I thumbed the gun button to give the Brownings a test squirt, Gilbert in the turret following suit.

'Hell of a lot of them', said Bill. 'Could be twenty.'

'Get off the sighting and amplifying reports, Bill, and I'll go in and give them our load.'

Not that it would be much use against surface ships. We were carrying an anti-submarine load of thin-cased hundred-pounders which would probably break up on contact with a metal hull. As we came nearer it was obvious that we had a most complicated situation on our hands, there being nineteen vessels all told. The convoy was led by six U-boats in line abreast about half a mile apart, and steering south-west as for England. Behind them, and on a slightly different heading, were six small vessels that could have been mine-sweepers, and behind those were a cruiser and six destroyers. It was a bit like the sort of exercise that they used to set us at the School of Maritime Reconnaissance – an unlikely assembly of vessels on a variety of courses and on an unlikely mission, your job being to give a concise and coherent report as quickly as possible. The obvious interpretation in this case was that they were the prelude to an invasion fleet. But why on earth were the U-boats leading? Surely they wouldn't sail into our minefields *ahead* of their mine-sweepers, which could have swept a clear channel for them!

Bill got weaving with the cipher machine, and as soon as our signals were acknowledged I went for the nearest U-boat, the most profitable target with our existing bomb-load. Spray frothed up his side as his ballast tanks opened, and I felt I'd got him cold. A few hundred yards before we got to him he disappeared, but his conning tower had left a big slick on the surface, so I wasn't worrying unduly. In a few seconds I'd drop my stick of bombs ahead of his track, with a good chance of doing him serious damage.

But incredibly, as we got to his approximate diving position there was nothing to see. Absolutely nothing except the opaque, heaving mass of sea. No slick, no shadowy shape a few feet below the surface, just *nothing* to indicate that somewhere below was a thousand tons of the most deadly weapon of the war at sea.

Bemused by the lack of a target, I took comfort that there were still five more U-boats to have a go at. As I went after No. 2, the mine-sweepers and destroyers put out a fair amount of light flak – light in calibre, that is, not in volume, which was considerable from a dozen assorted vessels. But again the U-boat vanishing act happened, and yet again. It seemed pointless to unload on a target I couldn't see, so a destroyer would now be the next bet. An anti-submarine bomb *might* get through their relatively thin plating without breaking up.

Then our gunner came up on the intercom: 'Messerschmitt 110, green one-five-oh. Closing in.'

With twenty times our firepower, and 100 mph faster than us, we were on a loser. I fled into the nearest cloud cover. Once there I realised that this could not be the end of the affair. I couldn't return home and say that a solitary 110 had driven me off.

'Bill, let me know when you've got the latest signal off, and we'll have another go at them.'

Was I mistaken, or did Bill look a bit crestfallen? It would be a relief – in a way – to know that perhaps his courage was ebbing, too, but neither of us ever brought the subject up, and he'd certainly shown no obvious signs of reluctance to engage the enemy as yet. I circled unhappily until Bill had sorted his signals out, then broke cloud and made off across the cloudless area in which the enemy sailed south-westwards, settling for a high-level attack on the destroyers. The customary dialogue between jittery pilot and intent bomb aimer ensued on the run-in, but Bill kept on muttering about something strange moving very rapidly over the surface of the sea a mile below.

'Stop nattering, Bill, and get on with aiming those bloody

bombs.'

'That's what I'm trying to do. But here it comes again. *Really* fast.'

More and more puffs of exploding anti-aircraft shells dotted the sky around.

'Tell you what, Bill, I'll turn up the taps. I'll take her in at 165 knots.'

'Oh no you don't.. I can't alter the bombsight settings at this stage ... right a bit ... bit more ... hold it ... left/left ...steady ... steaaady ... Bombs gone.'

About bloody time, too. I shut the bomb-doors and prepared for home.

'What's all this stuff you've been rabbiting on about, Bill, the fast-moving effort?'

'Damned funny. Yes! Here it comes again, sort of V-shaped. Take a look.'

I dipped the left wing, skidded on some right rudder and looked down between the port engine and the fuselage. And what I saw couldn't be mistaken for anything else. The optician, when he made my glasses, said he'd over-corrected them a bit to cope with future deterioration in my vision, and it was obvious that my eyesight with glasses was better than Bill's. I slammed the throttles into Emergency boost and looked for the nearest clouds – about four miles away.

'For God's sake, Bill! For the last few minutes you've been looking at five of the best-selling products of the Bayerische Flugzeugwerke ...109s, Bill! One Oh Bloody Nines. Five of the sods in Vic formation. You need your head seeing to, taking me over that lot like a sitting duck at my time of life.'

As I looked down in dismay, the first of our ten bombs hit the water near the 109s. Quite obviously, they'd become bored with circling their charges and were doing a sea-level beat-up of the ships to relieve the monotony. The succeeding line of waterspouts from the exploding bombs marched forwards towards the line of destroyers, the nearest being about fifty yards from one ship, but the 109s flew right through them.

One second they were jolly fighter boys cavorting after their leader; the next in the middle of ten waterspouts, any one of which could have shattered a propeller or a wing, and which made a mockery of their entire mission – the defence of their convoy from air attack. They were going to be a very cross bunch of guys as they came curving off the water in a split-arse turn to get at us, reminding me of a Walt Disney film of a stirred-up wasps' nest, the humour of the situation lasting a full half-second before my stomach went into its customary knotted-up ball. With the supercharger boost gauges reading an impressive 40 inches of mercury against the recommended maximum of 35$\frac{1}{2}$, the engines were getting a bit of a pounding, but they did their bit, and we made cloud cover several hundred yards ahead of the 109s, four very relieved people.

Bill disappeared into the nose for a few minutes and came back with his sandwiches and thermos flask.

'Steer 286 degrees magnetic. Want a sandwich?'

God, how could he do it? I could no more have put food into this dragging leaden stomach of mine than I could fly my Hudson to the moon. 'No thanks, Bill. Not hungry.'

'Remember that ham and butter from the torpedoed ship?' he continued. 'Now those were the days!'

My stomach was a sea of acid. I had to get Bill off the subject of food.

'Bill, please stop talking with your mouth full. And would you like to borrow my glasses next time we fly. Or perhaps we could have a whip-round of the crew to buy you some.'

'Not to worry. Just leave things to me and you'll be OK. You know, I wouldn't like to be those fighter boys when they get back to base. I'll bet Goering will come down from *Luftwaffe* HQ and personally bury his boot in each of those five arses, They'll end up flying desks for the rest of the war.'

I could well imagine it, and as I did the thought arose: it wouldn't be all that bad, really, to have to fly a desk for the rest of the war. There were far worse occupations when you came to think about it.

Three days later we found ourselves No. 5 of a barrel-scraping shipping strike, led by four of 224 Squadron. In miserable weather – low cloud, pouring rain and wretched visibility – we hunted up and down off Heligoland with little hope of success. Dusk was falling, and in a particularly slashing rainstorm, three Messerschmitt 110s overtook us a few hundred yards to starboard. In the rain, the forward visibility through their windscreens would have been as bad as ours, and they obviously didn't see us. They vanished, none the wiser.

Indeed, after watching the enemy disappear and bringing my gaze back to our own formation I found that I had lost them, too, so decided to pack in the useless quest and head for home. Then, out of the murk, pom-pom tracer rose up at us – we had fortuitously lighted on the ships we were seeking: If they hadn't opened fire we wouldn't have known they were there. But as it turned out it didn't matter one way or the other. By the time I'd done a three-sixty to make a bombing run the visibility had deteriorated even further, and we never found them again.

Next day, by way of a change, I *led* the shipping strike of the only four aircraft that could be spared from other duties. A 10,000-ton blockade runner, escorted by five flak ships, was sailing into the Skagerrak. (We found out later that she was the *Nordmark*, sister ship of the notorious prison ship *Altmark*, and, like her, a supply ship for commerce raiders.)

I had two other 233 aircraft – flown by Ather and Sgt Bailey – and Sgt Morrison from 224 Squadron. Ather and Morrison were fairly inexperienced, so I planned to attack in two pairs from opposite directions to split up the gunfire. When we found the convoy I would waggle my wings, and Ather and Morrison would break away to fly to the seaward side of the ships. Sgt Bailey and I would attack from landward, which I considered to be the more dangerous, as it was nearer the *Luftwaffe* fighter bases. Five minutes after we separated we would both turn in to attack. There was a layer of stratus cloud with its base at about 2,000 feet, into which we could pop after dropping our bombs.

The usual atmosphere of a bombing run against a well-defended target built up in my skull as we ran in, and I wished I'd never heard of Wagner and his damned Valkyries. As the 20 and 40 mm hate reached out at us from the six ships, *The Ride of the Valkyries* ran through and through my head. I couldn't shut it out of those smoky fingers and winking gun muzzles, and felt aggrieved that it was Wagner's compatriots who were hurling this load of shit at us. And anyway, Valkyries hadn't got to fly three or four hundred miles to get home.

And where, when you came to think of it, were Ather and Morrison, who were supposed to share this gunfire with us? Half a mile to go, and every gun firing at us. Nothing going out to sea. And just *look* at this group of 40 mm trails. If one of them comes through the windscreen marked 'Dopey Edwards' I suppose bloody Wagner will provide the usual clash of cymbals as the thing goes off in my face.

And if Bill doesn't get shut of those bombs soon I'm going to give him a piece of my mind. Or press the 'Jettison' button on him. That'll show who's in charge, prissying about with that bloody bombsight of his. Do him good. Wake his ideas up a bit.

'What's that? I *am* holding her steady. A hundred and forty bloody knots at fifteen hundred bloody feet, and if you can do any better come up here and try. But don't look out of the window, you crazy Kiwi, or it might put you off a bit.'

'Say again. *Bombs gone!* Good old Bill, good old bloody Bill. Bomb-doors shutting. Try and mark the stick. Sgt Bailey's, too, if you can spot them.'

But what on earth's that thud and vibration? And why am I in a screaming climbing turn? And why am I looking down through the roof of Sgt Bailey's cockpit? And he looking up at me in such a puzzled way?

And Bill's jubilant call of 'One hit' doesn't seem all that important really when you look out of the window and see a yard-wide stream of vaporising petrol streaming from under the port wing.

We'd been hit in at least one tank.

I put the Hudson right way up again, and Sgt Bailey fell in on my port wingtip. A fuel check showed that we'd lost about a hundred gallons of petrol, and Bill's navigation revealed that we'd probably have to ditch about twenty miles short of home. Fortunately, we now had Air Sea Rescue in our patch, and after an exchange of signals we received the happy news that the high-speed launch was leaving Tayport for our expected ditching position.

When we were safely away from any likely fighter interference I brought Gilbert out of the turret, as the Hudson would trim better that way and it might save the odd gallon of precious fuel. He came forward and sat on the main spar, occasionally getting up to stand alongside me to chat. He produced his sandwiches and munched contentedly away, the acid biting deeper into my gut at the mere sight of it. He was in a choir at St Andrews, and was concerned that if we ditched he would miss their public performance that night. 'You're off your rocker, Gilbert, if that's all you're worrying about', I thought. (Though didn't express.) He didn't seem to have any idea of what lay ahead if we had to ditch! When we hit the sea the Perspex nose of the Hudson would shatter, and tons of water would be rammed into the fuselage. There would be no avoiding that yard-wide, seventy-knot torrent that would smash into the stairs, some to be deflected sideways at me, the rest to continue into the cabin, where the crew would have their backs to the bulkhead against the shock of hitting. We would come to rest nose down and flooded with water, and they would have to jettison the door, which contained the precious dinghy, and get out before we sank. I would probably be slightly better off, as my emergency exit was immediately above my head. As long as they deployed the dinghy correctly I could slide down the wing into the water and clamber aboard.

'You know, sir,' broke Gilly into my train of thought, 'after the war I'm going to join a full-time choir and sing all the time.'

He took another bite of his sandwich. The acid bit deeper. Did he *have* to eat in front of me?

I got my own back. 'Hasn't it struck you, Gilbert, that there's probably no 'after the war for *us*?'

Gilly's open face dropped. I'd certainly succeeded in ruining his day. I felt a bit of a shit, and ran an instrument check, which revealed that we were about to run out of petrol on our third tank. I hastened to make amends.

'I'm running this tank absolutely dry, Gilbert, so we may end up with a temporary air lock. As soon as you hear the slightest sign of an engine cut get to work with the hand petrol pump.'

The port engine spluttered, and Gilly got cracking. The

starboard engine followed, and apart from the hiss of the slipstream an eerie and uncomfortable silence reigned. After a very long five seconds the port engine banged and stuttered its way back to full power, followed a few seconds later as the starboard engine came on song again. And we had lost only 300 feet in altitude.

But we could still run out of gas. I pushed the carburettor controls even further forward to weaken the mixture and save fuel, the cylinder-head temperatures going well into the red.

Bill came out of the nose and gave me his latest navigation check.

'Jesus! You're running the engines hot. Look at those cylinder-head temperatures!'

'Bugger the cylinder-head temperatures.'

'If you say so', said Bill. And we flew quietly on.

He broke the silence. 'I'll go into the cabin and check on the carrier pigeons. I've got a message all ready to fill in our time and position of ditching, and will let one of them go before we hit the water.'

'And don't forget to bring the other pigeons into the dinghy …'

'Land ahead', cried Gilbert, and the coast of Fife came up, to smiling faces all round.

'Well, Gillie, I hope you're in good voice for the Hallelujah Chorus tonight. I'm sure they'd have missed you if we'd dropped in the drink.'

After landing we looked at the damage – obviously from a 20 millimetre – and realised how lucky we'd been. You could put your head through the hole in the bottom of the fuel tank, which held 143 gallons when full. I'd checked its contents before I went in to attack, and it held 100 gallons, which left a 40-gallon airspace above the petrol. Fortunately, the shell had exploded within the 100 gallons of petrol, where there was no free oxygen, so no explosion or fire had resulted. Had it penetrated those extra few inches into the vapour space the resulting explosion would probably have blown the wing off.

At the debriefing Sgt Bailey said that he had had one near-miss with his bombs, so it looked as though we could have done the *Nordmark* a fair amount of damage.

Though at a price – the other two aircraft did not return.

The 50% casualty rate did nothing for my morale, and the irony was that I had given Ather and Morrison what I thought was the safer option, but it hadn't worked out that way. They'd obviously met serious fighter opposition on the other side of the convoy.

The next week something important must have been expected, as we did six routine patrols looking for something which I've forgotten about. Thankful that they were without incident, the feeling of depression weighed more heavily on me each time I flew. If the next shipping strike produced 50% casualties again the luck had to run out some time. The last time *Scharnhorst* had put to sea in our patch the Hun had put an umbrella of thirty to forty fighters over her, and we'd lost Feeney and Wallis.

We landed from the sixth trip to find a message in my office: all four of my crew members were to report to the Medical Officer in the morning, which seemed a bit odd. In peacetime we'd had regular, and strict, check-ups, everyone laying off the beer for a couple of days, jogging round the aerodrome and that sort of thing. All ideas of emulating the versatile sparrow, who could both fornicate and fly, were dropped for the time being so that we could enter the medical in tip-top form.

If I was going to have a medical in the morning they would test my vision, and a sense of lightness pervaded my being at the thought that inevitably they would find out I was short-sighted, and so would automatically ground me. But say they didn't do the eye tests? I wondered if I could arrange to pull my glasses case out of my pocket when I took out my handkerchief to make sure they copped me.

But as I looked at Bill stowing his parachute into his locker the depression returned, because I knew it just wasn't on. Physically, Bill looked as fit as a fiddle, and hadn't any easy let-out that I knew of. The old conviction returned – if you didn't do your job properly some other chap had to go out later and do it for you. I was back in the machine.

Next morning Bill and I went to Sick Quarters. I was in first.

'Morning, Dopey. Take a seat. How're you feeling?'

'Good enough, Doc.'

'How many operational hours have you done?'

What an odd question for an MO to ask!

'Not absolutely sure, Doc. Five hundred, maybe five-fifty. I could find out from my log-book if you need to know.'

'No, that'll be enough for my purpose. Now, how are you eating nowadays? Any problems?'

How on earth did *he* know?

'A few.'

'What did you have for breakfast?'

'Didn't have any, Doc.'

'Will you be having lunch?'

He seemed to know quite a bit about me.

'Not really sure.'

As he pursued the subject further I found myself thoroughly enjoying the routine of discussing me to the exclusion of all else – it was quite an absorbing subject. Then he produced something startling out of his hat.

'Those of you who've been flying since the Norwegian Campaign started are to have a rest from operations. You'll go to a convalescent home for a week or two before being posted to a training unit, for example. It'll be for about three months, then you'll return to an operational squadron again.'

Happiness! No more red-winking guns and tracer trails, no more splintery crashes of bullets going through the fuselage, no pressure waves blowing in your eyes and cheeks, no more cannon-balls. I'd see my 22nd birthday.

Perhaps even three meals a day! And perhaps the nightmare would go. Compounded of a mixture of my crash into the River Eden and Bill's near-miss on St Andrews' beach the day after our night trip to Hamburg, it was occurring with increasing regularity. With its nose pointing skywards, the Hudson was fully stalled and sinking rapidly into the estuary. Endlessly it sank as my stomach, with its customary cannon-ball, floated up in the weightlessness of the stall, the Valkyries pounding away in my skull, and the volume ever rising as the hellish stall got even worse. Then the dreadful, but welcome, CRAASHH of the cymbals that came just before we hit the estuary, at which I woke up, sweating, my stomach a ball of pain.

Was this really going to end for a while?

'Gosh, Doc! You really mean that. A three-months' rest!'

'Pukka gen. All of you who've been at it since last year are getting it.'

I passed Bill as I left the MO's office. 'You'll never guess what the MO's got up his sleeve for you, but I'm sure you're going to like it.'

Yet as I walked back to the mess I had an uneasy feeling that I might be running away from my responsibilities. Still, a rest would be a nice change. *Nice change!* What an understatement! It was going to be great! Weren't the birds singing loudly today. Wasn't the sun shining beautifully. Must be the first sunshine we've had for weeks. Boy, what a wonderful world!'

Before lunch a fair-sized group of us were nattering contentedly with pints in our hands, but also in a reasonably subdued manner, as the majority of the mess weren't in our fortunate position. Those pilots who'd joined as casualty replacements in 1940 still had some time to go before they were due for a rest. A three-ton truck took us to an under-used Army convalescent home which had been set up at the Hydro in Dunblane, near Stirling. Here we were joined by other Coastal Command crews from 269 Squadron up at Wick and 220 from Thornaby, our old peacetime station back in 1937.

We had our own – rather Spartan – rooms, all the carpets having been stripped out, but who cared? There was an indoor swimming pool.

The hot August days drifted past as, further south, the Battle of Britain reached its climax, familiar names of former term-mates from our flying training schools making national headlines as the Hurricanes and Spitfires tore into the enemy. I don't suppose that anyone in England really visualised defeat, and in common with many we found ourselves thinking of the opposing rates of destruction of aircraft in a way analogous to the cricket scores until, as pilots, we realised that this was not, indeed, a cricket match, but a slogging battle in which fighter boys were dying and being worn down as we had been.

I decided to get away, and managed to borrow an autocycle and some petrol coupons. Armed with my ration card, and with my emptied gas-mask case stuffed with the minimum of kit, I puttered away in the general direction of the Western Highlands, and revelled in the peaceful and impressive scenery. To my great disappointment, on the second day the engine seized, due, I suspected, to the fact that a filling-station had put neat petrol into the tank of my two-stroke instead of a petroil mixture.

Sadly, I pushed the machine to the nearest railway station, and settled down to a wait of several hours. When the train came in I put the autocycle in the guard's van and clambered into an apartment, to find that one of the two occupants was an ex-Medical Officer from Leuchars, the other a friend of his. From the flying-boat base at Oban they were coming to spend a 48-hour whooping it up in Stirling. Both were equipped with a travelling pack of a bottle of whisky, which they generously shared with me, so the journey became a very pleasant one. Our compartment was of the non-corridor type, and the noise level became such that any traveller opening the door at the numerous stops rapidly changed his mind, slammed the door and sought more peaceful surroundings. Such a spontaneous party had the inevitable result that we all got gloriously tight in a real, happy RAF binge. Alas, we reverted to type, and dredged up from our memories those half-forgotten dirty songs that I don't think any of us had sung for a couple of years or more.

'The donkey is a queer bloke,' sang the Doc in his somewhat powerful voice, 'And very seldom gets a poke/But when he does he lets it soak/As he revels in the joys of copulation.'

The engineer officer and I struck up the idiotic chorus: 'Cats on the rooftops/Cats on the tiles/Cats with syphilis/Cats with piles/Cats with their arseholes wreathed in smiles/As they revel in the joys of copulation.'

Before we could follow with *The Cruise of the Good Ship Venus* – whose figurehead was a whore in bed, the mast a rampant penis – a hammering on the wall indicated the displeasure of the occupants of the next-door compartment, and we had to cool it.

The Doc, contrary to my naïve conceptions of the standards

of behaviour of his noble profession – Hippocratic Oaths, General Medical Council and all that sort of stuff – was exceedingly fond of women, and appeared to regard his peacetime practice as a recruiting ground for bedmates, having a very practical approach to the matter.

'You see, Dopey, it's a great help being in the profession', he said, belching whisky fumes complacently. 'When you consider that every woman who walks into my surgery is going to take her knickers off at some time or other it's a bit of a pushover, isn't it?'

I was forced to agree, and regretted that the WAAFs with whom I came in daily contact – the MT drivers, cipher officers, clerks and so on – had no such obligation to remove their knickers in order to carry out their duties. Evidently, I was in the wrong job.

The train decanted three well-intoxicated types onto the platform at Stirling, and we parted company. For me there merely remained a five-mile push with my seized autocycle, a physical effort which did much to evaporate the almost neat whisky which was circulating in my veins.

A few days later the Group Medical Officer came to see us all. My interview was an informal affair, sitting out on the grass in the sunshine and chatting to him as he made a few notes on his pad.

'Right, Edwards, that's fine. You'll go back to your unit on Thursday pending a posting, probably to an Operational Training Unit. It's going to take some time to sort out all your postings, so you'll have to go back to your unit and hang around for a while. But no operational flying, you're not to do any of that.'

I hope my grin didn't show.

'And keep an eye on that ulcer of yours', he continued.

'Ulcer, sir?'

'You've got an incipient duodenal ulcer. Just watch your diet and it should clear up fairly soon. Go easy on the alcohol, too. Not good for ulcers.'

Never a rose without a thorn! But who cared? Three months with not a 109 or armoured ship in sight, a tracer a chap who worked in a drawing office, and perhaps back to a Pimms No. 1 on a Sunday morning!

Next day we went back to our units and were sent on a fortnight's leave. On my return my posting still hadn't been sorted out but I was till commanding 'A' Flight, and felt my position acutely as I organised the youngsters' flying details while frigging about doing things like air tests of machines coming off inspection or damage repair. But the North Sea was certainly quieter now, as also was the air fighting in the south. It looked as though the Battle of Britain was over.

At last my posting to a Navigation School came through, and I could leave my present difficult appointment as a non-flying Flight Commander. The peacetime custom of a send-off party in the mess had more-or-less vanished with the war, as our type of squadron could be called on at any time of the day or night, so I made my farewells the night before as best I could. I was catching a train at 11 in the morning, a decent time of day when the mess would probably be empty, so I could creep away without embarrassment, a kind of rat deserting a sinking ship. I rang the transport section to confirm that transport would be taking me to the station.

'I'll just check, sir', said the Flight Sergeant. 'Yes. Here it is – Flying Officer Edwards, three-tonner at the officers' mess, 10.30.'

'Three-tonner, Chiefy? There must be some mistake. A fifteen-hundredweight would do.'

'No, sir, it's a three-tonner that's been ordered. It'll be there at 10.30.'

Ah well, it seemed a bit large, but it would do.

On time, the Albion turned up at the mess and my batman put my luggage into the back as I climbed up into its high cabin. No one had seen me go, for which I was grateful, as I left them to carry on with their war. How things had changed in the five months since we all met those Heinkel 115s off the Norwegian coast on 5 April. No. 233 was a very different squadron now, hardly recognisable as the unit that had started the war. A lot of chaps had gone – Robinson and Godfrey, Mike Clarke and his second pilot, whose name I couldn't even remember now.

Evans, McLaren, Yorke, Feeney – our second-in-command – Wallis, Dunn, Wicht, Ewing, Buchanan, Horan, Paton and Immelman, Sgts Hallam, Bousfield, Ather, Crabtree and Cotton. I couldn't really remember them all. And as many from 224 Squadron. Then double the number, because a wireless operator and gunner went down with each aircraft.

It hadn't been an Agincourt, this Norwegian Campaign of ours, but perhaps we *could* call ourselves a band of brothers of sorts. Certainly, a bond had been forged between those of us who had survived. Despite the stupidity of war, the cruelty, pain and bereavement and so on, a *rapport* had been created between those of us who had survived, and with all other fighting men who had faced similar dangers. In my experience it was obtainable in no other fashion. It was unique, and was to last for the rest of our days.

The driver was speaking. 'What?'

'We're here, sir. Leuchars Junction.'

'Thanks, Corporal. Give me a hand with my kit, would you?'

He grinned as we walked round the back of the truck and swung down the tailboard, when the reason for the three-tonner became obvious. The back of it was full of 233 Squadron types, and a few 224 as well. It looked as though all the off-duty pilots were there. They jumped down, grinning and slapping me on the back.

'We just came along to make sure you hadn't pinched the mess silver, old horse.'

In a chattering band we pushed and jostled onto the platform, and eventually the Edinburgh train came in. A compartment door was opened, bodies swarmed in and stowed my kit and they shoved me in after it. I let down the window and tried to say something appropriate to the noisy mob of well-wishers, but it was fairly impossible to have coherent communication. But I did manage a bellowed 'So long, Bill' to Bill Tacon. I'd come a long way with him, and he'd never once let me down. I hoped I'd done as well by him.

The train pulled away, and I kept my head out of the window until they all vanished. As I pulled up the window and sat down I realised that the only other occupant was an attractive young woman sitting opposite me. I thought that I, or some of my well-wishers, must have been treading all over her toes or something, as she was looking at me in an odd sort of way.

And then I realised that I was feeling a bit tearful, and thought 'How nice of them to come and see me off like that. How damned *nice*.'

I hid behind my paper, and eventually started to read it. Yet again there had been negligible air activity over the South of England. It really looked as though the Battle of Britain was over. How relieved those fighter boys must be! Maybe the Hun *had* thrown us out of France, and now Norway, but it looked as though they'd been held to a draw in the Battle of Britain.

I'd be back.

At least, I thought I would …

Chapter Five

Flying a Desk at Home and Abroad

I was posted as a Flight Commander to a Navigation School at Cranage, in Cheshire, where the pupils were pilots destined for Bomber Command and were doing the short navigation course as an essential part of their basic flight knowledge. In the air they put into practice all that they were being taught in the classrooms, and we 'taxi-drivers' provided the aircraft for them.

Cranage was newly built, a cluster of hangars and wooden huts set in a sea of mud. It had no concrete runways, just a single airstrip of coarse steel mesh laid on the grass, and the taxi-drivers were a mixture of newly qualified pilots and those of us on rest from operational flying in the Battles of France and Britain, in Coastal Command, etc.

Sadly, we flew the unexciting Anson, but there was a pay-off for me in that Cranage still used the pre-war system of aircraft maintenance. Operational squadrons had long converted to a centralised workshop system, as the flight commanders were too occupied with the flying side of things to cope with aircraft servicing as well. But here, under the old regime, I had a dozen Ansons, and it was an added interest having to provide ten serviceable aircraft every day, juggling the flying hours of each one so that not more than two were on routine inspections at any one time.

A new pilot was posted to my flight: Peter Wakeford had flown Fairey Battles in France before Dunkirk – one of the quickest ways to Paradise ever invented by the RAF – and it turned out that he, too, liked flying as many types of aircraft as he could lay his hands on. And, as so many of us did after the

Battle of Britain, he also wanted to be a glamorous fighter boy. It would be nice to shoot the hell out of somebody else for a change, instead of always being on the receiving end, although I *did* have some reservations on the subject. I don't want to hurt people's feelings or destroy reputations, but at my Flying Training School there was no doubt that those chosen for fighters were drawn from the less cerebral of our term-mates, the unspoken theory behind it being that if they made a mistake and crashed they would kill only themselves, whereas those of us intended for twin-engined aircraft could have up to four lives in our hands.

Despite this reservation, in December 1940, I submitted the following application to the CO for a posting to a fighter unit:

From: Flight Lieutenant G. Edwards.

To: Officer Commanding, No. 2 School of Air Navigation, RAF, Cranage.

Date: 12/12/40.

Ref: Posting to a Fighter Unit.

Sir,

I have the honour to submit this application to be posted to No. 422 Squadron, which is forming and which needs pilots.

I have 1,375 hours' flying experience of which 70 hours are at night. Of this total 540 hours are operational flying on Hudson aircraft, and includes a certain amount of fixed-front-gun fighting against Messerschmitt 110s, 109s, Junkers 88s, Heinkel 115s and the Dornier 18K flying-boats.
*

I have also done 40 hours on Blenheim 1 aircraft.

At the beginning of August I was taken off operational flying, and after the 4? months' rest feel fully fit and I am very keen to get back to it.

---

* Not strictly accurate. It implies more front-gun experience than I actually had. I was on the attacking side against Heinkels and Dorniers, but only once managed a shot at a Messerschmitt which had been foolish enough to overshoot me after his attack. I winged over and managed a highly satisfactory squirt at him as he broke away.

If it is not possible to get into No. 422 Squadron I should like to be posted to some other fighter squadron.

I have the honour to be, Sir, your obedient servant,

The CO returned it to me marked 'Not Approved'.

Peter Wakeford was made Airmen's Entertainment Officer, and had contacted the Mayor of the local council, pointing out that a few hundred men had been dumped in the middle of Cheshire seven miles from nowhere, and had little to do, so between them they organised a dance, the entry fee being sixpence for the airmen, but a shilling for the girls, which seemed a bit rough on the delicate creatures who were about to be thrown to the lions.

Pete appealed to me: 'I can't control a hundred airmen in a situation like this by myself. They'll rape half the women in Cheshire if we don't keep 'em down. Give me a hand with them.'

On the night, Pete and I watched the airmen de-bus from three-ton trucks and followed them into the hall, three sides of which were lined with seated girls, hands demurely in laps and eyes cast down, though flicking hopefully upwards at intervals. The band was doing its best, the Mayor was circulating, but in the far corner the brutal and licentious airmen cowered, refusing to budge, despite the heady effects of free lemonade.

'Pete, we've got to break this up. Grab yourself a girl.'

But I had a slight problem. After those 109s so nearly jumped me due to my short sight, I had bought myself a pair of specs, but I couldn't wear them in public or I'd end up flying a desk. With my blurred vision I didn't want to land myself with the local equivalent of a Russian tractor driver, so started a close-range tour of the perimeter, looking for someone more on the lines of the Venus de Milo. Blurred face came and went, then into focus swam a vision of beauty – sparkling eyes, kindly smiling face, masses of auburn hair in a page-boy bob and a figure that made the Venus de Milo look a real slag. (When we were better acquainted, if I squeezed hard enough to make her squeal I could get the fingers and thumbs of my two hands to meet round her 21 in. waist.)

Her name was Christine, and she was obviously very kind, as

she didn't flinch when I told her that mine was Dopey. We got along fine, and she broke off her engagement to a chap in the Army, who came galloping home on compassionate leave to sort things out. In answer to his question, 'Is there another man?' she was able to give an honest 'No', as I hadn't yet popped the question, but even as she said it there was a roar of mighty engines as I beat the place up at roof-top height, and her mother ran out onto the back lawn waving the dishcloth. He took the hint and gave up. It must have been a savage blow to the Army to lose both Dunkirk and Christine in so short a time.

She was very much an individual character. On our way home from an evening-dress dance we had stopped the car for a bit of snogging, and I thought things were looking promising. But she suddenly broke things off, got out of the car, and started doing cartwheels in the middle of the road. The frou-frou of her frock as she whirled in the light of the dim wartime headlights was suddenly interrupted by a wail of despair as her shoes flew off and vanished into the darkness. I got my torch and searched the muddy ditch for them as she touched up her nail varnish by the light of the dashboard lamp. When I delivered her back to her parents I was glad of the black-out, as the poor hall lighting helped greatly in concealing my mud-spattered uniform, which made me look as though I'd been raping their daughter.

We now had a new CO, so in April 1941 I put in a second application for posting to fighters, which he approved, presumably passing it higher up the echelon, though nothing ever came of it. But a chance to provide a bit more leverage in any future request arose when Peter Wakeford, a born fixer, discovered that I had to fly to Sealand on official business.

'Sealand! There's a Spitfire Operational Training Unit there. Old So-and-So's a Flight Commander there. Know him well. He was in the Battle of France with me. He'll probably lend us a couple of Spits.'

Tempting. I *did* like flying different types of aircraft, but my current steed, the Anson, was hardly a ball of fire, not ideal training for a 1,000 hp fighter. However, I took comfort from the fact that no one in his right mind would lend me one.

With my business at Sealand finished we walked into Old So-
and-So's office. 'Pete,' he exclaimed, 'never thought I'd see *you*
again. Thought you'd copped it at Saint Omer that god-awful
Thursday.'

They yarned about their pre-Dunkirk days, while I tried hard
to hold my end up with the comparable difficulties in the
Norwegian Campaign – Messerschmitts, and that sort of thing.

'What can I do for you, Pete?'

'Could you lend us a couple of Spits for a quick whip-
round?'

'They'll have to be Mark Is, I'm afraid, all the Mark Vs are
busy.'

The horror of the situation struck me when I realised that I
couldn't ask for what any normal person would want to see
before flying a new aircraft –the 'Pilot's Notes', which told you
what all the knobs and things in the cockpit were about. I'd held
my corner so well in the matter of Messerschmitts and so on that
it seemed to be assumed that I was one of the mob. I staggered
out to my allotted Spitfire and ferreted around the unfamiliar
cockpit until, in all decency, I could keep the ground crew
waiting no longer. And I must have pressed enough of the right
buttons as, with a shattering backfire and cloud of smoke, the
Merlin engine banged into life.

There was also an Elementary Flying School at Sealand, and
I had to zigzag my way through gaggles of Tiger Moths before
finding a straight take-off line and shoving open the throttle.
She unstuck easily, though I nearly ended up with hiccups, as
the undercart on this early model had to be pumped up by
hand. The Spit was quite sensitive on the elevator, and I found
that as I pumped the lever to and fro with my right hand I
developed a compensatory opposite movement of the left,
which was holding the joystick, my stomach reacting
accordingly. But the gear locked up eventually, and after
spending five minutes' homework on the cockpit contents I flew
off to shoot a line at my home, a few miles away in North Wales,
coming down to fifty feet in the valley a mile away, where I
could not be seen, then rising with a roar of mighty engines as
though from the very earth itself for the customary treetop runs

over the house, to let my mother and the village know that the lad was flying Spitfires nowadays.

Then off to my uncle's house a mile away, which, disappointingly, didn't produce quite the same reaction. Auntie Edith did not appear. But her dog, on the third run-past, tore panic-stricken down the garden path and disappeared under the wing root. With the advantage of viewing the matter from above I found it remarkable just how far forward in front of his ears Tinker's hind legs could reach before they thrashed down on the power stroke.

It was to be some time before I got the whole story. Auntie Edith thought the Germans had arrived, so spent the time under the kitchen table, and the demented Tinker had shot off to the farmhouse next door and got rid of his anger by shaking seven chickens to death, for which Uncle Dick had to pay.

Back at Sealand I pumped down the undercart without getting hiccups, the flaps went down with a hiss and a thump, and I selected a Tiger-Moth-free area for my landing. But as I throttled back for the approach the nose of the Spitfire pitched *up*, not down, as did most of the stuff I'd flown, completely blanking off the view ahead. Unbelievably, I carried on with a blind approach, Tiger Moths flitting backwards as I swept through them like Boadicea, but the Gods were merciful, nothing got in the way, and I pulled off a daisy-cutter landing.

'Funny thing, sir,' said the fitter as he helped me out of my gear, 'that's the first time I've seen a Spitfire brought in on a straight approach like yours.'

I staggered away, bemused by my lack of intelligence. Hadn't I seen film after film with Spitfires cleaving in on that graceful, curved approach which gave a clear view of the landing area? I think there was, in the back of my mind, the idea that after only forty-five minutes on the type, if I once chickened out and did an overshoot it might become the first of many, until I did one final panic-stricken landing as the fuel ran out.

But I'd got away with it, thanked Old So-and-So, and Peter and I rattled back to Cranage, hugging our guilty secret to ourselves. No fruit like stolen fruit.

But even hardened members of the criminal classes have to

draw the line somewhere, and when Pete produced the 'Handling Notes for the Hurricane Aircraft' that he'd borrowed from the night-fighter squadron the other side of the aerodrome, and suggested a quick whip-round in a Hurricane, I was on safe ground.

'No dice, old boy. Read out order No. 3 in the Pilots' Order Book to me, will you?'

'Er, Navigation School pilots are forbidden to fly the fighter aircraft.'

'Clear enough? Now just get on and let me have that aircraft serviceability state I asked you for.'

'OK,' said Pete, 'but as we happen to have the book here we might as well have a good look at it. Just for information.'

No harm in that, of course, and having spun through them an automatic reaction took over, and we found ourselves cycling over to 96 Squadron's dispersal, where we went into the usual spiel with Verity, one of their Flight Commanders, who'd recently knocked down a couple of Heinkels in the Battle of Britain. A laid-back New Zealander and a kindly fellow, he signed the Authorisation Book. But for only one aircraft. I pulled rank on Pete, and flew off in what was to be V7621's last-flight-but-one. It handled easily and, sensibly, the nose pitched down for an easy landing. After refuelling Pete took it up, and I lay down at dispersal in the pleasant sunshine waiting for him to return, which he did about forty minutes later. But it looked as though he was in trouble, as he kept circling round and round the aerodrome. The general opinion was that he couldn't get the undercarriage down, obviously not having taken in from our hurried spin through the Handling Notes that in case of hydraulic failure one kicked two locks sideways, which released the wheels to fall part-down under their own weight. One then shook, rolled and generally horsed the aircraft around until the wheels locked.

But by the time he was contacted on the radio the engine had caught fire, and as he opened the cockpit hood the flames swept right into the cockpit and into his face, and that was the last thing he remembered. We watched as the Hurricane dropped out of sight in a flat glide behind the woods, and arrived on the scene to find a fiercely burning Hurricane, the roar of the fire punctuated by the snap, crackle and pop of exploding ammunition, and Peter, a bit burned about the face, staggering around in circles fifty yards away.

After a short spell in hospital Pete reappeared fit for duty and fit, of course, for the Court of Enquiry. Used as I am to the slings and arrows of outrageous fortune, who was I to complain when I was dragged into the sordid affair to state that on its previous flight the undercart had given no trouble, and to reveal that not one, but *two* Navigation School pilots had been involved in the outrage. Even worse, studies of their log-books revealed that both pilots had also made what appeared to be unauthorised flights in Spitfires a few days before.

Our actions were 'Viewed With Displeasure' by an exalted personage, especially mine as a Flight Commander. I don't know what Peter's eventual fate was, as he was posted away soon afterwards, but I lost nine months' seniority on my promotion to squadron leader, a bitter psychological and financial blow. I don't think that so a harsh punishment was intentional, I was just a victim of the system whereby officers were assessed for promotion at quarterly intervals, and six months of good conduct had to be demonstrable before the recommendation would be considered. I perhaps, or obviously, deserved not to be recommended when the next three months came up, but then had to sweat out the additional six. They were very expensive flights.

But they did at least get me, a twin-engined pilot, into the cockpits of those two charismatic fighters. So whenever anyone in later years asked me if I had ever flown Hurricanes and Spitfires I could answer very truthfully about the former, since my last flight in the UK before going out to Burma in 1944 was in a Hurricane, as was one of my first flights when I got there, and I usually managed to gloss over the fact that the Spitfire flight was in the singular.

I was delighted when a Hudson was delivered to Cranage to introduce the pupils to more modern instrumentations, and as the only other Hudson pilot on the station was an apparently indifferent ground instructor, it became my personal aircraft. It was very nice flying a machine with whoomph again, and fun demonstrating some of its modern gadgets to the pupils. This later Mark had fully feathering propellers, which greatly reduced the drag if an engine had to be shut down, and so, demonstrating this to my audience one day, I hit the feathering button and showed just how well the Hudson flew on one engine, especially one with feathering props. But when I hit the button a second time to unfeather, the prop stayed obstinately where it was. Time and again I tried, but always with the same result. It would not budge. Among my passengers was an engine fitter, and thinking that a fuse might have blown somewhere we set about the lengthy business of changing every fuse in the aircraft, but still without result. The Hudson flew perfectly well on one engine, but there were seven lives at risk, so just in case the other engine got stroppy I decided to jettison 400 gallons of petrol. With that lot overboard she flew easier, and I landed without further incident, keeping up enough speed to run straight onto the tarmac, where my Flight Sergeant came on board to find out what the trouble was. With the port engine still running to keep up the hydraulic pressure, I explained.

'Starboard unfeathering's on the blink, Chiefy.'

He pressed the button. And it unfeathered! Just like that!

Fortunately, I had the evidence of the fitter and the others to back me up, but the Station Commander heard about one aspect of it and sent for me.

'You dumped 400 gallons of petrol! Do you realise that the ship that brought that petrol into the country had to run the gauntlet of all those U-boats in the North Atlantic.'

This to a Coastal Command pilot!

'It relieved me of a ton in weight, sir. I had six passengers on board.'

He grunted in an unimpressed fashion.

Maybe I *shouldn't* have applied to leave his unit for a fighter squadron so soon after joining it. Or been caught out flying the Spit and Hurricane, of course, though that was entirely Peter's fault

One of my pilots, lost in bad weather, force-landed in a field in Wales that was so small that it couldn't be flown out: it had to be dismantled and sent back to me by road. Unfortunately the crew detailed to do the job from the nearest Maintenance Unit were unfamiliar with the Anson, so solved some of the problems they encountered by cutting through every control that led from the cockpit to the wings. Fuel pipes, electric leads, control cables and mechanical connections were hack-sawed through with abandon, and when my Servicing Flight Sergeant took delivery of the wreck he nearly wept. It took my servicing crews over a month to get that machine flying again, weeks during which the aircraft serviceability state of No. 1 Flight was usually one below that of the three other whiz-kid Flight Commanders down the road. Bad for my reputation.

So when another of my pilots, again lost in bad weather, force-landed out in the sticks, I took a maintenance crew with me and went to see for myself. I paced the field, which was a bit on the small side, and at the upwind end were a ditch and some 22 kV power cables lining a busy road. But I reckoned I could get her out, lightening the machine as much as possible by taking out the guns and ammunition and by draining away most of the petrol into the ground. (If the Station Commander had ever found *that* out he'd have had my guts for garters.)

Revving up against the brakes, I let go and set off for home, but when almost airborne I hit a soft area in the grass, which slowed the Anson down. But I had passed the point of no return. There was not enough field left in which to come to a stop. I wallowed on, the semi-stalled left wing dropped, and the undercart on that side hit the ditch an enormous clout, which flung me into the air *underneath* the power cables, so fortunately they did not short-circuit via my metal aerial and fry me alive. I shot across the main road at an altitude of about six feet just a few yards in front of a horrified car driver, wallowed across the next field, got up to flying speed and flew uneasily back to Cranage.

I landed as gently as possible, as I suspected that the port undercarriage had taken a bit of a pounding, as indeed it had. As it collapsed I went into the customary Catherine-wheel routine on starboard wheel, tailwheel and disintegrating wingtip, complicated by the fact that just before it came to rest the wretched thing tipped up on its nose, and dug into our steel-mesh runway with a whiplash-inducing jolt. I rode it like a bucking bronco until it came to rest, then baled rapidly out of the side window and slid down the wing, a quicker exit than having to clamber up the 30-degree slope to the door, now about ten feet above the ground. And anyway, it might have caught fire!

But the venture paid off in two ways: (i) My Flight Sergeant had the machine flying within the week, so my serviceability record remained unblemished, and (ii) I decided that that would be the last time I put undue consideration for Air Force property before my own safety, especially as Christine had now accepted my proposal of marriage, the pair of us now being known in the mess as Dopey and the Body Beautiful. I had to grab her while the going was good.

The wedding was to be a white one, and I nearly ruined it as, through circumstances within my control, they said, I ended up with a bit of shrapnel in my left eye-socket and had to go into hospital five days before the ceremony to have it removed.

But our wedding went off very well indeed, though my eldest brother Tudor, who *had* transferred to the RAF after all, did not attend, as he couldn't get leave from his light-bomber squadron. Christine and I went off on our honeymoon in Llandudno, on the way back calling in on my mother, who met us with the sad news that Tudor had been shot down and killed at Rotterdam five days earlier. My widowed mother, very kindly, had not wished to spoil our honeymoon, so had not told us about it – a very brave gesture, and a sad end to our honeymoon.

Navigation School pupils did not fly at night – that part of their training came later – so we taxi-drivers had to keep up our own night-flying skills with periodic practices. On my first stint as OC night-flying the Met forecast was good, so as soon as I had sent off half a dozen of my pilots on some simple circuits and landings I took to the air myself, and was worried to find that there was no horizon – that faint indication of where the sky ended and the earth began. This was no weather for tyros, as some of my pilots were, and I felt that there was no urgency in their training, anyway, as there would be other, better nights. I landed, and cancelled night-flying.

The first pilot to land after me came into the crew room and asked, 'Why's night-flying cancelled?'

'No horizon,' I said, 'too dodgy.'

'No horizon! There's a perfectly good horizon!'

And so said all the others as they trooped in.

'You're quite happy with it?'

'Perfectly happy. It's a lovely night.'

So I had to restart the exercise, but when I got airborne I still couldn't see anything much except the lights of the flare-path, and as I still had the better part of an hour left to complete my detail I steered a compass course for that distant haze on the horizon where the railway marshalling yards at Crewe were lit up as long as there was no air raid warning.

I circled that haven of light for half an hour, hoping that the balloon barrage had been lowered for the night. (One of my pilots, in daylight and below cloud, *had* hit one of the cables, but was lucky enough to catch it on one of his propellers, which severed it, the balloon ascending to heaven knew where, and no doubt mystifying the balloon crew when the cable came snaking down without having brought down an enemy aircraft.)

When my time was up I steered a compass course back home and landed thankfully.

But I had been rumbled. The Medical Officer sent for me and gave me a real workover. Not only did I fail the night-vision test abysmally, but the short sight that I'd successfully concealed since those 109s jumped me in 1940 was revealed. As was my potential duodenal ulcer. Such a miserable physical record could have only one conclusion – I was grounded – and for the month of November 1941 my sole log-book entry is 'Am to be made O/C latrines and pig-swill disposal.' And in the New Year: 'Still flying a bloody desk.'

But in March 1942 I clawed my way back to flying again, though with the second-rate 'Non-operational/Home Service Only' category.

With Christine expecting a baby, I gave thought to the future.

The big step was to regain a full flying category, but that wasn't on the cards yet, and in order to convert my Short Service Commission into the Permanent Commission which I wanted I had to qualify in one of four specialities – navigation, armament, signals or engineering. With my fascination with guns and antique pistols I chose the five-month armament course, to be taken at Manby, in Lincolnshire.

During a slow and chilly cross-country railway journey the hot water bottle which Christine carried on such travels soon went cold, and we arrived in the tiny Lincolnshire village as dusk fell, finding digs in an old farmhouse which had no electricity or running water. Christine immediately opted for a bath to get warm and clean again.

'Follow me, dear', said the farmer's wife, and led us across a cobbled yard to a cold and dusty outhouse. Having shooed the chickens out, she indicated a bath full of onions in one corner, and a brick fireplace holding an iron boiler in another.

'Take the onions out and put them on the table over there, then fill the boiler with water. The pump's in the yard, and a dozen buckets should be enough to fill it to the three-inch level which is all we're allowed nowadays, as I'm sure you will remember. The kindling's over there, and when the fire gets going keep it stoked with coal – the shovel's over there. It'll be hot within the hour, and when you've finished, pull the plug and the water will run away through that drain hole in the wall, but make sure it hasn't silted up or you'll flood the place.'

'Sounds like hard work', said Christine after she'd left. 'And it's freezing cold. And there's no lock on the door – the pig man could come in at any time. And just *look* at that hole in the wall! Rats could get in through that. RATS! And I want to come out of a bath smelling of roses, not onions.'

She opted out, and next day found a house in the village which sold her a bath for a shilling, as long as she brought her own bath-towel, and I took baths in the mess. A week or two later we found permanent digs in a lovely old house called Upp Hall, set on a wooded rise which was actually within the perimeter wire of the station. I could have cycled to work in three minutes along the taxi track, but the Station Commander, an ex-Guardsman, decreed otherwise. I had to leave Upp Hall via the nearest gun post, cycle down the farm track, turn left on the main road and re-enter at the guardroom half a mile away, like everyone else. But Upp Hall was worth it: I don't suppose the sun shone every day, but the ambience was such that it just seemed like it. Run by Kathleen Milsom, the other rooms were let to an air gunner and his wife, Joan, all five of us sharing the kitchen, and there was a large lawn on which we could relax and have friends. Kathleen's pedigree Labrador bitch was in season, but it was ordained that she was not to enjoy marital status until a suitable sire had been found, none of the local punk dogs being allowed near her. So when Kathleen went off to market one day the girls were given strict orders that the yard door was to be kept firmly shut at all times. Christine was ironing in the kitchen when a wail from Joan brought her out into the yard, to see a distinctly down-market dog glued firmly into Kathleen's up-market bitch. Shouts, roars, shrieks of laughter and a tug-of-war that threatened the dogs' internal organs had no effect, and with the bus due at the end of the lane any minute there was no time to lose. Fortunately, the third bucket of cold water did the trick – the protagonists parted, the dog was chased away, and the girls set about drying the bitch with their bath-towels. By the time Kathleen returned she was asleep under the kitchen table and had dried off.

After we'd left Manby, we heard on the grapevine that the bitch had produced six very variegated puppies, not one of which would have been admitted to Crufts.

Early in the course I received some really bad news from Cranage – my personal steed, the Hudson, had crashed. Before I left I had trained up WO Salter, a very reliable man, to take over as the Hudson pilot, but as we'd all found to our cost in 1939, the Hudson could be very tricky if mishandled. Salter had stalled on approach and spun into the ground, killing eight people. Four of my former pilots died in that crash, including George Seal, our 'old man'. The 28-year-old George, a solicitor in civil life, had been a leavening influence on us younger men in the flight, and his wife was expecting her first child.

One evening we were sitting out on the lawn as dusk fell, when engine noises came from the west. The droning became louder, then incessant. Above our heads, dozens of heavy bombers were climbing for height as they headed for Germany. It went on and on for a very long time before the sound of the last engines faded away to silence. It was obviously a very heavy raid, and on the news next morning we had the explanation – it was the first Thousand-Bomber Raid. In large part it was a propaganda exercise to let Germany, Italy and the world know that we could do it. But it also explained a matter that had been the buzz of the mess for some days. A week or so earlier the Station Commander had been ordered to provide two fully operational aircraft and crews, to be drawn from the ex-bomber crews on the armament course. These aircraft would not be the mighty Lancasters, as we hadn't got any at Manby: they would be the smaller and older twin-engined stuff. But there's a world of difference between the one-hour training sorties that we did at Manby and a flight of hundreds of miles into enemy territory. You need reliable engines, for one thing. A ginger-headed flight lieutenant called Woods was allotted an elderly Hampden for this operation, but when he tested it there was a horrifying magneto drop on one of its engines, so he put the aircraft unserviceable until it was cured. It came back from workshops in little better shape, so he put it unserviceable again. With the same negative result. And yet again. In the end he refused to take the aircraft, and asked for a better one.

There wasn't one.

So the Station Commander, himself under stress I suppose, for having to produce two operationally fit crews from a training unit, *ordered* him to take it. Woods refused, a bold moral decision for a flight lieutenant, having to face down an officer three ranks above him, as his stand could so easily be demolished by an accusation of cowardice. His case was that in view of the dubious competence demonstrated by the aircraft's servicing engineers it was well on the cards that his second engine might go on the blink, too. Or it could be shot out. In which case the chances of returning were remote.

'If I'm given a serviceable aircraft I'll go, sir.'

The case was referred to higher authority, and I think Woods was awarded the benefit of the doubt, though I'm sure it wouldn't have done his promotion prospects much good.

Such a scene might well have developed at other training units, I imagine. The making-up of those numbers for the possibly propaganda-led thousand-bomber raid obviously led to a fair amount of barrel-scraping. The other machine sent by Manby did not return.

My dislike of flying as a passenger had increased, and early in the course I had approached the Chief Instructor with the plea that as Coastal Command pilots were also trained navigators, bomb aimers and stand-by air gunners, could I possibly be excused the relatively elementary air exercises, at the same time economising on staff pilots by flying the aircraft myself? Very kindly he agreed.

But he was posted, and the new one checked the records and had me on the mat.

'Edwards, you've not flown a single exercise since you've been here. What's the meaning of it?'

He didn't go along with my explanation, and from then on I was to fly every one. Unfortunately, the next trip was in a Hudson, that tricky machine in which the inexperienced Salter had taken eight people to their deaths a few weeks before. How much experience had this fresh-faced young lad now settling himself into the driving seat? My unease grew as I went down the steps into the nose to prepare the bombsight. And when the eleven hundred horsepower of the port engine bellowed into life the same horsepower of panic took over. It thrust me up the stairs, elbowed me past the other students in the cabin, and out onto the tarmac. There was only one haven – Christine and Upp Hall. I pedalled madly – and illegally – round the perimeter track and more or less flung myself into her surprised arms ...

'What happens now?' she asked later.

'An officer of similar rank will come along and place me under arrest.'

'Then what?'

'Dunno. My only defence – and not a very good one – is that I'm not chickening-out of the air. I'll fly anything I can get my hands on. But only as its pilot.'

The arresting officer was an unconscionable time a'coming, and the hours ticked slowly by.

In fact, he *never* came, and I slunk back for the afternoon's lectures to find that the other pupils had covered up for me, one of them dropping my detail of practice bombs. Or maybe the Wing Commander just gave me up as a bad job, and very kindly never detailed me for a passenger flight again.

A few weeks later I qualified as a specialist armament officer, and having now sweated out my penance for the illegal Spitfire and Hurricane flights, at last my promotion to squadron leader came through, and I was posted to a bleak east-coast station. I sent for Christine, and we found a furnished house to rent. It was a long cycle ride to and from the aerodrome, but this was well compensated by the fact that the house came with the unheard-of luxury of a housemaid. I suppose Ellen would have been about 14 or 15, and she was a resourceful girl. When Christine was doing the ironing and Ellen was washing-up one day, the front door burst open and a soldier flew down the corridor and into the kitchen. He flung off his battledress top and dived under the table, where he proceeded to wriggle out of his trousers. While the girls felt that it was unlikely that he would rape them, they *were* alarmed, an alarm that turned to mystification when he cried, 'Can you give me a pair of your husband's trousers?' Christine kept the hot iron in her hand as a weapon of self-defence, but the man was *pleading*, not threatening.

'My husband's in the Air Force, so blue trousers won't be any use to you. Anyway, why d'you want them?'

'I'm deserting.'

'*Deserting?* In the middle of a war?'

'Not really deserting, mum. My older brother joined the Navy, and I wanted to do the same, but they called me up into the Army. Wouldn't listen to me. I'm going to desert, lie low for a bit, then re-enlist in the Navy.'

This put a different complexion on things, and the girls sympathised. But a trouserless desperado could still be a danger, so Christine made sure the iron in her hand was still hot.

Then Ellen, with great presence of mind, said 'I'll just go and scrub the front doorstep, mum', and left the kitchen. Out in the street she met a military police patrol.

'Have you seen a man in uniform recently, miss?' asked the sergeant.

'I don't know about a uniform, but we've got a soldier with no trousers on in the kitchen.'

'He'll do.'

The patrol swarmed into the kitchen and hauled the cowering man from under the table.

'Now then, lad,' said the sergeant, 'what the hell d'you think you're doing, taking your trousers off and frightening these ladies?'

'I want to join the Navy, Sarge.'

'We know all about that, son, but you're in the *Army*. And your unit's warned for overseas. Deserting your unit when it's due to go off on active service is a serious crime. Get dressed.'

Christine took the sergeant aside. 'What will happen to him?'

'Well, like you've heard, mum, he's done something really serious – could get him two years, at least. But we've already checked on his records. His brother *is* in the Navy, and doing well enough. It's not for me to say, but I think his court martial would believe him. He's got to be punished, of course, so his unit will go overseas without him. But he's a machine-gunner, and God knows the Navy will have need of them. I think they'll discharge him from the Army when he's finished his punishment, and call him up immediately to re-enlist in the Navy.

The sad little cortège left the kitchen.

Her baby expected soon, Christine went back home, going into a maternity home which had been evacuated out into the country to escape the Manchester blitz. On one of the walks that she and another expectant mother took, they passed an American Army unit located in the grounds, from which issued the customary wolf whistles that now, sadly, are politically incorrect, and much missed.

'You know the saying that the Americans are overpaid, over-sexed and over here', observed the other wife. 'They're certainly over-sexed if they shower wolf whistles on pear-shaped, waddling women. We'll come this way again.'

On 30 December 1942 Guy was born. I managed to get a 48-hour pass to go and see them, but unfortunately was on a detachment on the east coast, miles away from Cheshire, so couldn't get hold of one of my own aircraft. I had to fly as passenger in an elderly Rapide biplane piloted by a chap who looked about 17 years old, wearing a jaunty jockey-cap pulled rakishly over one eye. He was obviously a devil-may-care type who was making a statement, and not the grizzled veteran that I would have preferred. The machine also had no wireless set.

As we crossed the Pennines the starboard engine failed. Then we ran into a snowstorm, and I was mightily relieved when we let down into relatively good weather on the Cheshire plain and reached our goal, Sealand, of Spitfire fame. The pilot put the flaps down and made his approach, but with oodles of landing space still available he decided he was overshooting, and opened up the good engine to go round again – an act of pure insanity in a Hudson, which would have spun out of control into the ground. As the Rapide fluttered and shuddered its way round the circuit I made my peace with the world, and took comfort from the fact that though it looked as though I was about to leave this world, Guy would carry on the – fairly common – family name.

But we made it, and thumped to earth.

'See you all on Monday, 08.30 prompt', said the pilot before we dispersed.

But I wasn't risking a second attempt on my life. 'Many thanks for the trip, old boy, but I'm going back by train.'

I got to the maternity home in the wilds of Cheshire, walked a mile across a pleasant snow-covered park, and met up with Christine again for the first time in six weeks, and Guy for the first time ever.

Sadly, Christine's father died a few months later, but at least he had had the pleasure of seeing and handling his grandson. He was a very gentle and kindly man.

I was posted to Long Kesh in Northern Ireland – later the Maze

Prison – as Armament Training Officer, being joined whenever possible by Christine and Guy. Christine has always regretted that she has not been in the services, to wear a glamorous uniform like so many of her friends, but in my estimation, the women married to servicemen had a much more difficult furrow to plough, so this would be the time to mention the unsung part that Christine and so many other women played during the war.

Before the war she had qualified as a commercial artist, and had lined up a job in Harrods' advertising department, but when the war started her father had become so ill that she transferred to war work in a local factory to help pay for his expensive pre-NHS medication. Then she landed a much more suitable job as a fashion designer for an American clothing firm, operating in England but exporting to the States for the so-necessary Lease-Lend finance. But when *I* turned up she became a camp follower, though a perfectly respectable one, being married. Like many other service wives, she followed me round as often as she could, an existence designed to tax women to breaking point. On marriage, a memory bank appeared to be triggered at Air Ministry, doubling the rate at which married men were posted from unit to unit. If it was suspected that life at a Lincolnshire airfield was proving to be relatively comfortable, a posting to Cornwall could be arranged, followed by one to the North of Scotland when it was discovered that the wife was pregnant. And they didn't want a robust young woman to do a 500-mile journey with four changes of train: they wanted one suffering from morning sickness. And with the corridors of troop trains crammed with soldiers with their haversacks, kit-bags and rifles, a trip to the loo could be a traumatic experience. She made endless journeys to many of the units to which I was posted, tramping or cycling in unfamiliar territory as she hunted for houses or digs to rent. Twice within a few weeks of finding accommodation I was off on the next posting, and she would have to return to her mother's yet again, before being summoned once more to some outlandish place.

On one trip in a non-corridor coach a fractious Guy was bellowing for his next meal, but it just wasn't done to breastfeed in public in those genteel, though barbarous, days, and she was hoping that the next change of train wasn't too far distant, so that she could vanish into some awful station loo and feed him. But when he started clawing at her cleavage in a *very* determined way a percipient naval officer caught on and said, 'Right, chaps. Up with your newspapers.' Christine fished in her blouse, and Guy shut up.

At Long Kesh I had a stroke of luck. I already had a fair collection of antique muzzle-loading weapons, and I found that the barracks of the Royal Ulster Constabulary was just down the road at Sprucefield. What with the Troubles and all that they had hundreds of confiscated firearms there, among them antiques. After writing to what seemed like every government official except Winston Churchill, I got permission to visit the barracks, and to choose from that Aladdin's cave of treasures, from flintlock duelling pistols to the latest automatic pistol. But I would have to pay for them. They would be two shillings each – 10p! I bought twenty.

Then fate struck another blow. All three of us were now living in a pleasant dig within cycle ride of the aerodrome, but I was finding it increasingly difficult to pedal the distance, especially against the wind. I realised that something odd was up. Was I inheriting the complaint that caused my father's early death? I went to see the MO, and we had a long talk.

'Come and see me again in two days' time.'

'Edwards, we are sending you to Littleport for a while', he said at that interview.

'Any idea what they fly there?'

'They don't fly. It's a psychiatric unit …'

'*Psychiatric unit*, Doc! What the hell for?'

'We think you would benefit from it.'

He spoke at length, and what he said was humiliating.

Apparently the heavy casualties we'd received in the Norwegian Campaign had got under my skin more than I'd realised. Unable to pedal a bicycle against the wind, for God's sake!

The Nutcracker Suite at Littleport, as we called our ward, held a varied selection of patients, chiefly aircrew, though by no means all. And there wasn't the slightest doubt that we were all slightly ashamed of ourselves. But we were cheered to find that one of the patients himself was a psychiatrist. If *he* doesn't know what's wrong with him, we thought, then perhaps there's some hope for us. It was only much later that it clicked. He was obviously a mole, noting our every word and action, which is why I imagine that we were diagnosed relatively easily. (We had never heard of Post-Traumatic Stress Disorder in those days.)

The conclusion reached about me was that with a wife and child, another on the way, one brother dead and a widowed mother to help – and Christine's mother also now a widow – I was imbued with a greater desire to live for my country than to die for it. Not a very flattering assessment, but I wasn't entirely alone in this. Many of us never *really* understood those RAF heroes who went on and on and on, dying showered with medals. But when I left Littleport I was again able to ride a bicycle against the wind, though they wouldn't upgrade my flying category: I was still 'Non-Operational Home Service Only'.

Looking back after all these years, I am immensely grateful for the sympathetic treatment we weaker members of society received in our war, compared with those of our fathers' war, when teenagers who had suffered nerve-wracking day after day of dreadful bombardment in utter squalor were shot for 'cowardice'. Which today makes me so disgusted with our present-day politicians, not one of whom has ever fought in a war to my knowledge, economising on money by passing on repatriated wounded servicemen to civilian hospitals in the UK. In Littleport we were with others of our kind; we knew the jargon; were more-or-less at home, and could swap similar experiences. But those coming home from Iraq and Afghanistan can be passed on to civilian NHS hospitals, where a man terribly burned while rescuing his comrades under fire can lie alongside a man recovering from a dog bite. And then be discharged into the empty civilian world to join the endless queue of patients on waiting lists that seem to go on for ever!

My unit moved to Turnberry, on the west coast of Scotland,

where the golf course had been turned into an aerodrome, and where Christine and Guy joined me in a pleasant furnished house with easy access to the shore. But the future Susan was being obstreperous, Christine developing a severe toxaemia. She was given an ultimatum: if the vomiting and other symptoms did not resolve in a week the pregnancy would have to be terminated. The future Susan must have heard this threat, so lay doggo for a while, and Christine started to improve, the real turning point being when the son of Mrs McDonald, our weekly cleaner, shot a wild duck, which she cooked and brought in to the patient, forecasting – accurately – that the toxaemia was due to 'a change of sairxxxx, Mrs Edwarrrds.'

My office phone rang. 'Guardroom here, sir, Corporal Sands There's a telegram for you, shall I send it up?'

I had a feeling.

'No, read it to me please, Corporal.'

'Er… Regret to inform you that your brother, Trooper E.E. Edwards, Royal Scots Greys, killed in action.'

So Teddy had now followed Tudor. He had survived the Western Desert without a scratch, then all the way up Italy with the 5th Army, with only a spell in hospital with malaria, before coming back to the UK in preparation for the invasion of Europe. His tank had brewed up in Normandy, and he has no grave.

I rang my mother, now with her second son killed in this never-ending war.

When we were young, Teddy told imaginative stories, holding my sister Gwen and me in thrall as he related the adventures of Phineas the Walking stick, and his anthropomorphic band. He wrote, and illustrated, an account of a football match between our village and the next, our dogs winning 'paws down', the hero of the match being our sheepdog Alfonso, named after the recently deposed King of Spain.

Called up, he had trained as a wireless operator/gun loader in an up-market cavalry regiment equipped with Sherman tanks, attaining the rank of lance-corporal, and I remember a distinct feeling of sadness on reading one of his letters home, in which he openly criticised his officers as being remote and unsympathetic. I hoped – and I think knew really – that our wireless operators and air gunners did not feel the same way towards us pilots.

The crunch came when Teddy wrote a letter, censored by his unit of course – but which he had kept – showing it to me on our last leave together just before D-Day. When in the 8th Army, fighting Rommel in the Western Desert, he had written home that in the routine orders of his CO was the one that first thing in the morning all other ranks were to leave their tents, and within a circle of six feet around them, pick up each grain of sand, polish it, and replace it in exactly the same place. His colonel was cross, and sentenced him to four weeks' loss of privileges. Then he had a better idea – he got him posted to another unit.

Teddy reported to the Royal Scots Greys, his crime-sheet going with him, of course. Trembling before his new CO, he expected even more severe punishment, as the Colonel seemed to be taking an inordinate amount of time in studying the letter.

'Edwards, I confirm your punishment. Well deserved.'

'Thank you, sir.'

'Er, Edwards, have you ever thought of sending this letter to the editor of *Punch?* You might even get paid for it.'

Teddy felt much more at home in the Greys.

I was warned for service in the Far East, where the normal posting was for three years. This posed problems. The Japs were still driving us back in Burma, so it looked as though it was going to be a long war, and I would be leaving Christine, Guy, the unborn Susan, and two widows, my mother having already had two of her three sons killed. (This was before the American film *Saving Private Ryan* was made about an American widow who had four sons in the Army, three of them having already been killed, so great efforts were made to locate the fourth, and bring him safely out of action.)

The obvious solution was to draw attention to my medical category of 'Home Service Only,' but I wanted a Permanent

Commission when the war was over, so the fewer black marks against my name the better. So I said nothing, and went. Oddly, at the Embarkation Unit they handed me my medical documents, to be handed in to the medicos at Bombay.

In September 1944 our convoy left Liverpool for Bombay, being the first to go via the Suez Canal for about a couple of years, as at last we had the better of the German and Italian navies in the Mediterranean, previous convoys having had to go via the Cape of Good Hope. And it was while I was leaning over the rail and watching the 'white horses' break on the wave tops that I remembered that bulky envelope of medical documents in the bottom of my suitcase. I went back to the cabin which I shared with five others, broke the seal, and started to read …

With such a lamentable record there was little hope of a permanent commission. I went back on deck and flung them overboard. They vanished into the turbulent wake, and I became a first-class citizen again.

From Bombay I did a 3 ½-day train journey to Calcutta, where I fought my way onto an over-crowded Dakota transport and flew 500 miles north-east to Imphal, in Manipur, where the Japanese siege had at last been broken, and we were starting to push them back. I took over the job of Armament Officer of No. 221 Group, a close-support fighter/bomber group of about twenty squadrons attached to the 14th Army. We were equipped with fairly elderly Hurricanes and Spitfires, and the impressive American Thunderbolt that packed twice the bomb-load and gunpower of the Spits and Hurris. We also had some Mosquitoes, but these fast and modern aircraft were giving trouble, their glued wooden construction not standing up to tropical humidity, one of them having broken-up in mid-air, killing both the crew. They were sent back to India for modification, and they never returned to Central Burma during my time there: I think they operated from the Arakan, nearer to India, where a better eye could be kept on them.

In my new job I faced four big problems:

(i) The ammunition dump at Imphal had just blown up, probably sabotaged by the Indian National Army, who sided with the Japanese in their struggle for independence from the British Raj. This left 14th Army and our Group seriously short of reserve ordnance.

(ii) Our Spitfires and Hurricanes were having serious trouble in low-level bombing attacks – bombs were bouncing off the hard paddy fields and, their fuses then activated, were chasing after, and bursting dangerously close to, the dropping aircraft. (These weren't the famous bouncing bombs of Dam Buster fame: they were very unwelcome home-grown affairs.)

(iii) Bombs were hanging up on the racks after their release hooks opened, later to drop off haphazardly on friend and foe alike.

(iv) Though not lethal, this was frustrating in the extreme. A consignment of second-rate 20 mm cannon ammunition, already condemned as useless by the 2nd Tactical Air Force, had been adjudged good enough for us in the Far East. It jammed our guns for months.

But after a couple of days of delving into the rather full in-tray which my predecessor had bequeathed to me I felt the need of some fresh air, so went down to the airstrip and borrowed a Hurricane from one of the squadron commanders for a quick whip-round.

'You're not flying like that, are you, for heaven's sake?' he said as I prepared to climb in.

'Like what.'

'No water bottle, machete or revolver?'

'Er, no.'

He looked at me as though I were a halfwit and went back to his tent, returning with his webbing belt. 'Strictly on loan', he said. 'Never fly without this lot strapped round your waist. If you have to bale out if the engine conks or a Jap gets the better of you it could take you days to walk out of the jungle, and you could be in serious trouble without this lot.'

I was fully organised before I next flew.

To minimise the number of bouncing bombs I was to run tests with unfused bombs that had steel spikes a foot long screwed into their noses to make them stick in better. I found a dropping-zone clear of camps sites, etc., and as the Hurricanes would be dropping from about 200 feet with a fair degree of accuracy I stood with my two photographers about thirty yards from the target, one of them taking a shot as the bomb hit the ground, the other twenty yards to his left, to take a snapshot should any bomb emerge, which many did, as it turned out. As a bomb hit the ground showers of grit flew around, but we were getting the photographic results we needed, and it was fascinating watching the ground crack twenty yards on from the impact point, and the bomb – now minus its sheet-metal tail – emerging like a flying pig, tumbling end over end as it chased after the dropping aircraft.

There was a dodgy moment when one clown of a pilot mistook the instructions and came down tucked in closely to the side of another Hurricane as they came in for the drop, and not astern of him. I heard the click of the bomb-releases a hundred feet above and yelled to the photographers to beat it. The ground shook, and a shower of grit like no other we'd experienced before hit us. That much closer and we'd have lost our legs. But at least I'd ended up with enough photographic evidence to persuade the fighter boys to dive at much steeper angles to get the bombs to stick in.

But the Fates hadn't finished with me yet.

We ended up with two tons of unusable bombs, so I handed things over to an officer of the Royal Engineers, who was to blow them up. My armament manual recommended a safety distance of 400 yards for the disposal of such a load, *provided the demolition party was in a slit trench*. But the Engineers had only 120 yards of electric cable. And no spades to dig a trench.

'In that case, don't you think it might be a good idea to blow one bomb first,' I suggested to the RE, 'then tip the rest into the crater before blowing them all up. Much safer with such a short cable.'

'Awful lot of work in this heat, you know', he said, continuing to lay blocks of gun cotton on the pile of bombs.

We walked back to where the exploder dynamo lay on the ground, and he knelt and started to connect up the wires to the terminals.

'Look, if you're considering setting fire to that lot under these conditions, the RAF are leaving. Wait until we've gone.'

His reply was to twist the exploder key ...

First to arrive were blurred shards of bomb casings, skittering through our party with an enormous hissing noise, followed a millisecond later by a gigantic detonation that blew the wits out of the lot of us.

Gathering myself together, I was delighted to find that I did not *need* gathering together – every bit of me being in its correct place. My photographers, too. But not so one unfortunate Engineer sepoy. From the waist up he was the normal Jungle green of our uniforms; from the waist down a sea of blood. He had obviously been cut in two, and I waited for the top half to fall off. When it didn't I walked over to him. 'You all right, soldier?'

'*Teek hai*, sahib.' (Urdu for OK.)

'Well, if you're *teek hai*,' I said waving at the lower part of his body, 'what's all this about?'

He took one look, his eyeballs rolled up into his skull, and he fell down in a faint.

But when he recovered we found he was hardly injured – a piece of shrapnel had sliced neatly across the front of his elbow, opening up a vein which was spouting blood furiously. A make-do tourniquet had him on his feet in no time.

The Engineer listened fairly attentively while I analysed his parenthood, and we left the scene.

There were four or five attempts on my life in Burma, of which these two – nearly having my legs knocked off by a bomb, and then managing to evade being blown to bits – were the first. Only one of them was by the Japs.

I had to go to Kohima, about sixty miles to the north as the crow flies, though any crow would have collapsed with vertigo at the road I had to follow. Rough of surface, it twisted and wound through dramatic mountains, nearly all of them covered in trees, though I couldn't pay them much attention as I couldn't take my eyes off the road, where barely a hundred yards at a time were straight. The near-vertical slopes on the left were matched by vertiginous drops to the valley on the right, at the bottom of which a small river meandered. Small in appearance, that is, but close up it would have been large and slow and muddy. It was a road to be treated with caution, as a lot of traffic was coming down from Kohima, convoy after convoy of three-ton trucks with Indian drivers who either were extremely skilled or placed little value on their lives, and even less on mine, forcing me to scrape the Jeep against the rocks on one side or, far worse, edging me another foot towards that appalling drop into oblivion.

As I rounded a bend in more open country I had to brake to a stop, as a column of Nagas were crossing the road. Unlike the Burmese and Indians I'd hitherto come in contact with, they were jungly men, and seemed to have come out of the nineteenth century, the men being armed with bows and arrows, and blow-pipes, though the leader carried a sign of authority by way of a muzzle-loading musket which I wouldn't have fired for a gold clock – the barrel was paper-thin, and the broken hammer-spring had been replaced by a length of rubber tubing tacked to the stock and looped round the hammer. I duly admired his weapon, but felt that possibly the safest places to be when it went off would have been in front of the muzzle.

The women of the party trailed behind the men, and carried all the loads, of course.

During the war in Burma the Nagas moved round the jungle, evading both us and the Japs as far as possible, and we had all heard of a mysterious Englishwoman known as 'The Queen of the Nagas', who, as a young woman, had been left behind for some reason when the Japs had invaded.

She had lived with them for years, and finally been accepted as their leader. She was a bit of a battle-axe, according to one of my friends who knew her later, as I well imagine she must have been to be able to survive for years in such conditions. It is very sad to think that these fiercely independent people are being so savagely treated by the present vile regime in modern Burma.

When I got to Kohima I was appalled by the destruction. In that desolation of shattered trees and shell-holes not a single building seemed to have survived intact. My business finished, I took the mountain road again, but was now going with the general flow of the traffic, so it was easier, and much safer. I could now take more notice of my surroundings, and stopped at something I'd missed on the way up. In a rock-strewn clearing at the side of the road were a dozen wooden crosses, the graves of perhaps a platoon wiped out by the Japanese. I felt that they were an awful long way from home – as we all were, though we'd probably get there eventually. Years later I learned of the inscription on the war memorial at Kohima, the second most war-devastated place I ever saw: 'When you go home/Tell them of us, and say/That for their tomorrow/We gave our today.'

With the Japs now on the run, the 14th Army and our supporting Group moved their headquarters from Manipur, and over the mountains to Indainggye in Burma. Before we moved, orders were issued stating that RAF officers were not to take personal servants to look after them in Burma – there was a war on, etc. It wasn't as though we were mollycoddled at Imphal, but one didn't relish returning by air or road from hours of wrestling with problems miles away to have to make up one's bed, clean boots, wash through sweat-soaked jungle greens and so on. So I had shared a local Manipuri servant with three other officers, which didn't cost an awful lot, and meant a great deal to my comfort. But that was now to change.

I was put in charge of the RAF Advance Party, to go ahead with a similar Army outfit and turn a patch of jungle into a working campsite. I was issued with a 40 lb tent, and took it and my camp kit of canvas bed, chair and water bucket, and with other Army types on the same mission flew down to Indainggye, from where we were trucked a few miles into the jungle where, for camouflage reasons, the camp was to be pitched. I erected my tent – so small that one could not stand up in it – but at least, it was a hovel that I would not have to share it with anyone else.

By nightfall I had made reasonable progress in organising the RAF site, after which a field kitchen fed us the luxury of a hot bully-beef stew. But after the bracing climate of Imphal it was much more humid and enervating at Indainggye. It was our introduction to the jungle. Throughout the night, condensation dripped from the trees onto my canvas roof, and the morning was dank and misty. The jungle was certainly safer from attack by Japanese aircraft, but it was a depressing place to live.

I was shaving in cold water when a 14th Army acquaintance passed by.

'Good God, Gron! Is this the best you can do?'

'What d'you mean?'

'Well, slumming in a 40-pounder for a start. And shaving in cold water. Your servant needs a bloody good kick up the arse.'

'I haven't got a servant whose arse I can kick.'

I explained – 'Look, I know that your lot are called the Forgotten Army, but at least you *have* been forgotten. *My* mob, 221 Group, have never been *heard* of, except by our families back home.'

'Yeah, I suppose so. But if this is how the RAF goes to war you're crackers, the lot of you. Look, I'll send a few of my chaps round in a jiffy to give you a hand.'

Four West African soldiers appeared, with two empty oil drums, machetes, cord and fencing wire. They dismantled the tent and re-erected it with the tent poles supported on the drums, extending the guy ropes with cord. I could now stand up in the tent, but there was an 18 in. gap all round the base. So they laid into the surrounding elephant grass and bamboo with their machetes, and wove panels from it, walling in the bottom of the tent. Inside, they hammered four bamboo stakes into the ground and lifted my suitcase onto them. 'No more ants, baas', they explained.

The Army type came round to inspect progress, and from my palace of a tent I thanked him from the bottom of my heart.

'Hang on, they haven't finished yet. They've got to do the *ghusal khana*.'

'*A bath house!*'

'Yes. Won't take 'em a jiffy.'

Within the hour, six-foot-high panels of elephant grass were staked round my tent in an L shape, and my canvas bath laid in the completely private area. 'Maidenly modesty, and all that sort of stuff', said my friend. 'And I'd forget that bullshit about no servants if I were you. Hire some local lads.'

When the rest of my staff turned up they goggled at my palatial quarters, and we did what the kindly Army chap had suggested, recruiting Dey Ma and Mah San Sheyn, who stayed with us for the next two moves forward.

The jungle was claustrophobic, and it was a relief to go down to the airstrip and leap into the air, though my first trip had its moments. A particularly unpleasant disease called scrub typhus had broken out, apparently caused by creepy-crawlies in the grass, so we all had to wear heavy Army boots and gaiters to keep them out. I was to fly an Artillery officer to observe a raid by B24 heavy-bombers from bases back in India, and used a Stinson L5 light aircraft, which could operate easily from our small airstrip. But being a lightweight, it required a certain delicacy of rudder control which, with my clodhoppers, I just hadn't got. The airstrip was a fifty-yard-wide affair lined here and there with trees, and I made a dodgy swerve to one side of the strip, followed by a clodhopping correction to the other. To cries of distress from the back cockpit I zigzagged my way into the air. The gunner wasn't impressed.

The raid, appropriately called an 'Earthquake', was a softening-up process on an awkwardly-shaped Japanese strong-point before the infantry went in, and the gunner and I stood back a bit from the troops' start line. The first of the thirty-six Liberators droned into sight at 12,000 feet, and from each of their bellies a vertical line of a dozen 1,000 lb bombs dropped down, arcing into parabolas before thumping into the hills where the Japs had dug in. As the target disappeared in a cloud of dust the ground shook, and a second later the shattering noise of the explosions arrived.

The B24s turned north-westwards for their bases back in India, and the whole thing was repeated by the next two squadrons.

When it was all over the Major and I were assessing the damage, and as we walked back came across an unexploded thousand-pounder lying on the surface. With the kindly idea of easing the load of my old friends, the bomb disposal people of the Royal Engineers, I bent down and started to unscrew the fuse to disarm it.

'Er, that green-painted band round the fuse,' broke in the Major, 'I know more about shells than bombs, of course, but doesn't that indicate an anti-removal device?'

My God, so it did! How dim can a Specialist Armament Officer get! And I'd already unscrewed it one thread. If I'd carried on a few more turns it would have fired and blown us both to smithereens. With my heart in my mouth, I screwed it back.

'Thanks chum. I really owe you one. I'll return the compliment, and take my boots off for the flight home.'

Which was a relatively safe affair, as I have rather ticklish soles to my feet, and mystified the gunner somewhat with the cackles that accompanied any aerial manoeuvre. Eventually, the typhus scare blew over; I could wear shoes again; and flying became a much less dramatic.

We were having trouble with bombs 'hanging up'. The pilot would press the release button and the release hook would open, but instead of the bomb dropping off it would stay obstinately there, dangling dangerously off the open hook, to fall off at some unpredictable time later, usually on or near an Army camp, though one fell off as a Hurricane touched down on landing, the explosion killing the pilot. Nobody had yet solved the problem; it just seemed to be accepted as a normal hazard of Hurricane and Spitfire life, until the day that 37 Squadron shot up into the charts with a horrifying four hang-ups in two sorties, way above the normal. The AVM had me on the mat.

'Get down to Sadaung and sort this out immediately.'

'I'll fly down first thing in the morning, sir.'

'You'll go down now. By road. I've cancelled 37's morning sortie, and I want that trouble sorted out by midday.'

I wasn't looking forward to a night journey on vile and poorly mapped roads, so scrounged tins of bully beef and beetroot from the mess tent in case I got stuck somewhere, collected my bedroll, buckled on my gunbelt, and slipped my 30-calibre carbine into the clips beneath the Jeep's dashboard. Both we and the Japs had the habit of sending jitter parties into one another's territory to shoot up convoys, and vanish into the jungle again, causing a disturbance far in excess of the effort that had to be put into the operation, so I tucked the flap of my revolver holster open, ready for a quick grab, and laid the Jeep's hood flat on the bonnet to give me an all-round field of fire. The road was inches deep in gritty white dust which hissed away in a bow wave from the front wheels, and I drove through jungle devastated by artillery fire, shattered trees raising grotesque branches in the headlights which, as the Japs never flew at night, could be kept on full beam.

Rounding a corner, I was suddenly faced with two eyes glowing like coals, and by the twelve-inch distance between them it was obviously the biggest tiger in Burma. My most effective tiger-basher, though a pretty ineffectual one at that, was the M1 carbine, but there was no time to get at it. I crammed on the brakes, snatched my revolver from the holster and got off a hideously inaccurate double-action shot towards those eyes. I was already pulling off a second shot when the front wheels hit a rock with a crash that nearly up-ended the Jeep, that shot exiting through the front wing. As I spat out half my fillings I saw a beautiful little fox, inter-ocular distance fully three inches, leaping away into the ravaged jungle. Feeling a bit of an ass, I reloaded the fired rounds and carried on to the airstrip which 37 Squadron shared with another Hurricane squadron.

I managed to get an evening meal, then we all settled down to a detailed analysis of just why 37 was performing so very much worse than the other mob, no satisfactory conclusion being reached before we went to bed. Next morning I watched and grilled the armourers on every stage of their bombing-up procedures, and could find no fault with them. I had no alternative but to report this back to the AOC, who wasn't impressed with my performance. 'Oh, all right,' he sighed, 'I'll put them back as operational again.'

Early next morning there was the Burma equivalent of a knock at the front door as a muffled curse indicated that someone had tripped over one of the guy ropes of my tent.

'AOC wants to see you,' said his PA. 'Very pronto!'

I faced an incandescent boss. 'Edwards, 37 Squadron's had

even more hang-ups than yesterday. What the hell's going on down there?'

'I'm terribly sorry, sir, but I can't see *anything* wrong with their rearming.' And followed with a plea. 'Even back in India, sir, with all their research facilities, they haven't solved this problem yet.'

He grunted. 'Well get down there and try again. The squadron's grounded until it's fixed.'

I flew down to the squadron's airstrip – rather a rough one – to find an air of strain. The armourers, as far as the pilots went, were second-class citizens, and it was very sad to see this breakdown in a compact unit like a Hurricane squadron. The armourers went through their rearming again with unfused bombs, and pilots did circuit after circuit, before bringing their Hurricanes back to dispersal, where they were jacked up into flying position, and the release buttons pressed.

In all cases the bombs thumped to earth perfectly.

Then a passing pilot from the other squadron looked in. They lived at the other end of the airstrip, and took off and landed in the opposite direction from 37. He listened to pilots binding about having to do this chore in such heat from such a rough airstrip.

'Rough airstrip?' queried the visiting pilot. 'It's a smooth as a baby's bottom.'

'Baby's bottom my arse! It's like corrugated iron.'

A ray of hope shone through the gloom.

'You mean that? You really think it's a smooth airstrip', I asked the visiting pilot.

'I don't think it, I *know* it.'

I had an idea. 'We'll take a break for half an hour.'

I started up my own machine and taxied fast, the horrible surface punishing the L5's undercart, but I kept going, and sure enough, about half-way down the strip things got better. By the time I got to the far end the surface was as good as anything I'd flown from in Burma. Could 37 Squadron's end of the strip be contributing to the hang-ups? Bombs hung from the racks on a single hook, and were steadied from the buffeting of the slipstream by screwing down 'crutches' to prevent them moving too much. The standard method of crutching-down from time immemorial was to allow the bomb a 'reasonable' amount of movement, as too-hard crutching could result in jamming the suspension hook. So a possibility was that the battering 37 Squadron's bombs received on take-off was resulting in the relatively soft metal of the suspension lug partially welding to the hardened steel of the suspension hook. In which case we had to reverse the age-old policy of gentle crutching-down.

But first I had to see if I could *reproduce* a hang-up, a thing nobody had been able to accomplish in the past. Just off the airstrip was the wreck of a transport Dakota that had overshot the runway, and it would make an excellent aiming mark.

'Get two of your pilots to do six circuits and bumps each, then approach in line astern and drop their bombs on that Dakota', I told the Squadron Commander. 'I'll stand to one side.'

'Six circuits and bumps in this heat! They'll be panned out.'

'Then choose two of your least bolshie pilots. SIX CIRCUITS!'

They did as they were told, but with no positive result to show for it.

'We'll have to do it again', I said to the Squadron Commander.

He protested. 'You can't expect them to flog round endlessly in this bloody heat.'

'And I can't go back and tell the Air Vice-Marshal that an officer four ranks below him refuses to carry out his orders. Choose another couple of pilots, and let battle commence again.'

We did. Again without result. And only after a prolonged argy-bargy with the CO did he finally agree that it wasn't worth his commission not to comply. 'Third time lucky, you know, old boy.'

But when they came in for the drop the second time, No. 2 was off to one side, just like that other clot at the bouncing-bomb trials. As I sprinted for safety I heard the bomb-releases snap open against the noise of the engines, and three bombs thundered to earth in the usual shower of grit.

But the fourth one, thank God, hung up, so I didn't lose my legs.

All I could pray for now was that the bomb would not drop off in any old place in its usual fashion. And again I was in luck. When the machine taxied in to dispersal the bomb was still dangling from the rack, and stayed there while we jacked the Hurricane up into flying position to study the matter.

I had reproduced a hang-up! So I was not too hard on the dim-witted pilot. The bomb required a surprising amount of shaking and hitting with a clenched fist to dislodge it.

We re-ran multiple tests with increased pressure on the crutches.

And it worked. We had no more hang-ups that day.

I flew contentedly home and reported to the AOC. The order went out to all squadrons on forward airstrips to increase crutching pressure, and the hang-up rate decreased dramatically

Late in 1946 or '47, when I was a struggling university student, an OHMS envelope arrived for me. It was about the time of the Berlin Airlift, when some reservists were being recalled to active service, and I opened it in trepidation. If it was my recall it was going to set me back disastrously on my five-year course.

But I needn't have worried. It was a *Mentioned in Dispatches* certificate for services in Burma.

I am well aware that there are many more glamorous ways of earning a Mention, but in Burma I had never had to use my brain so much before, and the satisfaction of using my wits to overcome not only the hang-up problem, but all the others that bedevilled us out there, was very great, and it was nice to know that my ex-boss, AVM Stanley Vincent, had thought so, too.

I had to do an overnight road trip to an Army unit, and so, with the light failing, I pulled off the road into a clearing in the elephant grass where other travellers had also pitched their tents, and tucked into my bully beef. When night fell, quickly as it does in the tropics, I lit my Tilley lamp and settled down for a short read before falling asleep. I was awakened by a blood-curdling scream uttered, obviously, by the largest and hungriest tiger in Burma. I grabbed my thirty-eight revolver, a paltry weapon against such a beast – and prepared to sell my life dearly.

It's relatively easy being courageous when you've got something solid, like a wooden wall or a corrugated-iron sheet, between you and IT, but a flimsy sheet of canvas gives no confidence at all. And the beast wouldn't have to come through the door, it could rip its way through the tent wall with ease, grab me in its teeth and carry me into the jungle before tucking in.

After an agonising, and apparently endless, series of horrendous shrieks the animal had obviously fed enough, so had packed it in, and I dropped off to sleep again.

Until another chilling outburst indicated that it might want some afters. Hoping it would choose one of the other occupants of the site for that I eventually dropped off again.

In the morning I finished off the rest of the bully for breakfast and asked one of my neighbours if he'd heard anything unusual during the night.

'Only those bloody transport elephants. They let 'em loose to graze when they've finished work, and I think it's their way of showing gratitude.'

I felt a bit of an ass as I drove away

But those transport elephants did a great job in Burma, especially when the rains turned the ground into a quagmire. Fascinated, I once watched one for an hour as it rebuilt a broken-down bridge over a dried-up *chaung*. It picked up heavy teak logs from a stack alongside the road, and balancing them across its tusks, its *mahout* urged it forward to place them so very accurately in place with its trunk.

Chapter Six

Finishing the War, Coming to Terms with Peace

We moved to Monywa, which was open country, and a welcome change from the claustrophobia of Indainggye. Pitching our tents on the banks of the River Chindwin, we had refreshing swims to wash off at the end of each day, a much more pleasant environment.

Then one day the AVM's PA appeared at my tent. 'AOC wants to see you. Looks cross', he said.

I was there within the minute.

'What are you doing in Burma, Edwards?'

What an odd question!

'I'm your Specialist Armament Officer, sir.'

'I'll put it another way. What's your medical category?'

'I think it's A2B, sir.'

'You *think!* What do you *know?*'

'Er, it's A2HBH, sir.'

'And what do the 'H's stand for?'

'Home Service Only, sir.'

He waved an arm round his office in the bombed-out house. 'Does *this* look like home to you?'

'No, sir.'

How on earth had they caught up with me? I'd thrown my medical documents overboard in the Med.

'So you *knew* you weren't supposed to come overseas?'

'Yessir.'

'Very noble of you, Edwards. But has it occurred to you that if they send you home it will take your successor a month or more to get to know the ropes out here, during which time efficiency will suffer.'

'I'm very sorry, sir.'

'So you bloody well ought to be. You're to go back to Calcutta for a medical board. Well, what are you waiting for? Get off to Calcutta.'

'And good luck with the medical', he bellowed as I left.

Calcutta, 500 miles to the west, was only two hops in a Communication Flight's Harvard if I refuelled at Chittagong. But the Flight Commander was adamant.

'Take the Harvard away for three days! Not on your Nellie; there are *hordes* queuing up for it. Bum a lift in a transport Dakota.'

Dakotas were not my favourite form of getting around – someone else was doing the driving, there were no parachutes, and they were frequently over-laden. And the one allocated to me was a fair imitation of Dante's *Inferno*, being a casualty-evacuation machine with twenty wounded Ghurkas aboard, arms and legs in splints, blood-stained bandages, a few able to sit on the bucket seats, the rest on the floor.

The solitary medical orderly and I looked after the uncomplaining soldiers as best we could, holding their water bottles for them to drink, rearranging arms and legs and slings, mopping up and so on. I was relieved when we landed at Dum Dum and handed them over to proper hospital orderlies.

The medical board were not the Tartars that I had expected. True, they grabbed me by the balls while telling me to say 'Aaaah' (why this was done I never knew), made me hold my breath for agonising lengths of time, and punched me here and there and everywhere. But they accepted the plea that my glasses had coped with my short sight for the last five years, and that night-blindness wasn't a problem in a country where we never flew at night. They allowed me to stay, and would send on two pairs of bulky corrected-lens bifocal goggles which I never used, as my own specs were good enough. And the overnight hotel in Calcutta was sheer luxury – hot bath at night, and early-morning tea, enlivened when a large rat appeared through the hole in the wall where the bath water ran out into a gutter outside. With a whoop the bearer slapped down the tea tray, grabbed a heavy stick propped up in the corner – presumably there for the purpose – and clubbed at the fleeing rodent, which got away with ease. This lifestyle suited me, but the hideous poverty on the streets of Calcutta was very distressing, and I wasn't all that surprised when a *fakir* or whatever he was strolled naked down the street. Naked apart from his begging bowl, that is.

I bought a bottle of Indian whisky and joined the queue of hitch-hikers at Dum Dum airport, watching in dismay as over a thousand pounds of over-weight was shoved aboard the Dakota – and all those mountains to cross. But beggars can't be choosers, and I was vastly relieved when we thumped down at Monywa, where I cadged a lift from Colonel Smith, our American liaison officer.

'That wouldn't be a bottle of whisky you've got there, Gron, would it?'

'Indian whisky, Smithie, not Johnny Walker.'

'Would you be interested in swapping it for a dozen cans of beer?'

Cans of beer! As a morale-booster, and a very good one, too, we each got three *bottles* of beer a month, brought in by the transport Dakotas, an enormous logistic concession. And it was free, too: we didn't have to pay for it! There were very varied reactions to the beer's arrival, weak characters drinking it the moment they laid their hands on it, and spending the next few days pleading to buy bottles from those of us with more self-restraint, who for three days running would put a bottle into a stocking and leave it to cool in the Chindwin while we swam. And there was a tale, quite untrue I'm sure, that a teetotaller of high principals had been physically assaulted after he opened his bottles and poured them away into the sand, instead of giving them to the needy.

But the Americans obviously thought on a different plane from us, Smithie explaining that the Yanks got it in cans, not bottles. I did the deal, and with two of my assistants went fishing with our standard equipment of hand-grenades. The first explosions produced only disappointing tiddlers, so it looked as though it was going to be Spam again for supper, and as I couldn't be bothered taking the last grenade back I pulled the pin and tossed it in. Suddenly the water heaved, and a yard-long fish thrashed half-stunned on the surface. There was no hesitation on anyone's part: clothed or not, we all dived in and grabbed the first fresh meat we'd seen for ages.

Then an Army type who'd been watching the action made a suggestion. 'My bearer's the best cook this side of Chittagong', he said. 'His curries would blow your head off. Let's do a deal. Give me the fish and I'll get him to curry it for supper, and you bring the beer.'

I did the second deal of the day, grabbed some socks and took the beer back to cool in the river.

The meal was an absolute corker, which I have never forgotten. When the heat of the day had gone the four of us sat in our camp chairs round a glowing fire in the fading light and drank three cans of river-cooled beer apiece as we tucked into a fantastic meal of curried fish, the like of which I'd never had before, the curry fumes swirling round the inside of my skull. It was the best meal I'd had since leaving England. It didn't matter one little bit that the plates were of battered enamel! We owned the earth that night.

The Royal Engineers were at it again. When on my way home from sorting out yet another problem I was feeling like a bit of light relief from the eternal jungle stretching on all sides below me, so was pleased to find that a small river meandering ahead through the trees was more or less on my track home. As light relief I went down to treetop level, twisting and turning a few feet off the deck, and rounding a corner I came upon an RE fishing party on a raft in the middle of the river, but whereas I fished with innocuous things like hand-grenades, the Engineers had no time for such an inefficient system: they used dynamite. As I straightened out from the bend, a hundred yards ahead I saw one of the men throw something into the river, and I didn't need telling what it was. A huge waterspout rose from the water, and there was no way of avoiding it. Fearing for the wooden propeller of my little L5, which could so easily shatter, I hit it with an almighty crash that shook the machine into a shivering jelly. Thank God, the propeller withstood it, and I emerged shaken but unscathed the other side, to climb away to safety.

As a means of keeping skin diseases at bay my predecessor had bequeathed me some *pinki parni* tablets– potassium permanganate – which turned the water pink. Camp-kit baths were canvas affairs a yard square and five inches deep, and he'd recommended a teaspoon of pinki parni in each bath. A few weeks after getting to Monywa I ran out of it, and as there wasn't a pharmacist nearer than 500 miles, sure enough I got ringworm. Along with the other skin diseases that plagued us the standard cures were the dyes Gentian Violet and Brilliant Green. Aboriginal-looking men with blue and green faces now haunted the scene, one unfortunate guinea-pig having had one side of his face painted green and the other violet by his experimentally inclined Medical Officer. In one respect I was lucky, in that my ringworm was entirely below the belt, and only obvious when we went swimming, but I found it a demoralising disease as one never felt really clean, however much one washed.

Then things got worse: I started to itch *everywhere*.

'Scabies', said the MO laconically.

'What's that?'

'Oh, it's just dozens of little mites that burrow into your skin.'

'*Live* things? Creepy-crawlies? And *dozens*?'

'Well, thousands really.'

My skin was alive! I'd really joined the fellowship of the disadvantaged in that country so far from home.

It was decided to upgrade many of the staff jobs at this time – we heard that it was a ploy to get round the politicians at home, a means of giving servicemen a rise in pay without having every reserved-occupation trade-unionist up in arms demanding comparable increases. The Signals, Engineering and Navigation specialists all went up to wing commander, but not, unfortunately, Armament. My love affair with firearms meant that I'd made a very bad choice of speciality, and I remained a squadron leader.

As we advanced, getting further away from the supply bases

in India, more and more of our munitions were having to be flown in, the logistical strain exacerbated by the destruction of the ammunition dump, which had been destroyed just before I'd arrived at Imphal, probably sabotaged by the Indian National Army, a militant section of the Indian movement for independence from the British Raj. Within a few years India did, indeed, achieve its independence, but the nationalism of the INA was completely misguided, as they allied themselves with the Japanese in the expectation that when, by their combined efforts, the British were thrown out of India the Japanese would then hand them their independence on a plate. What a hope! They seemed to have completely ignored the evil way the Japanese had behaved towards the Chinese in the Indo-Chinese war. Only once did I see some INA prisoners that we'd captured, and they didn't really look like a bunch of cut-throat dacoits who would do you in at the drop of a hat. They just looked an unhappy collection of lost and inefficient souls.

Then someone at HQ South-East Asia, 2,000 miles away in Ceylon, had a really bright idea. He suggested that as the Japs were retreating and abandoning munition dumps we could ease some of our supply problems by using captured Japanese bombs. He'd liaised with the Americans in the South Pacific and had found someone to translate a captured Japanese armament manual, though when I first read it I felt that the translator had learned his trade after just a couple of nights with a Geisha girl in Trincomalee. But the orders were simple – when the next Jap bomb dump was captured I was to go down and assess the feasibility of using their bombs.

Meiktila and its bomb dump were duly captured, so I flew down in a Harvard, with Pat Ironside, one of my nuts-and-bolts men, and was met by the Wing Armament Officer. As we walked from the aircraft he said, 'Come and look at this lot', and took us to a slit trench, in the bottom of which was a dead Jap with an aircraft bomb held between his knees, and a brick in his right hand. He was a ground-borne Kamikaze, waiting for a worthwhile target to turn up before he walloped the fuse with that brick. Fortunately, one of our chaps had beaten him to it with his revolver.

In his tent the Armament Officer produced a selection of Japanese fuses of varying shapes, colours and sizes that he'd brought back from the captured dump.

'What can you tell me about this lot?' I asked him.

'Nothing really, sir. I thought *you* had all the gen.'

'Can you read Japanese?'

'Good Lord, no.'

I opened the manual and picked up one of the fuses sketchily depicted there. 'Is this one instantaneous or delayed-action?'

'Can't really tell.'

'Might it also have an anti-removal device?'

'No idea.'

My unease grew. The more I delved into this idea the less I liked it.

'What about the bombs themselves? Any problems?'

'Much the same as ours, except they have double suspension lugs.'

Great! Our bombs had single lugs. Their bombs would not fit onto our racks

'I think we can get around that one quite easily, sir', interjected Pat Ironside. 'The Engineers could run off adaptor rods with two hooks on one side and one on the other.'

I made a mental note that perhaps I might withhold Pat's recommendation for promotion the next time it came round.

'OK, let's get off to the dump.'

I drove along the Meiktila causeway, where three of our 500-pounders had cratered the road, leaving a chicane with just enough room to squeeze by. Then half a mile further on an Army captain stepped out of the bushes and waved us down.

'Going far?' he queried.

'Just to the Jap bomb dump.'

'I wouldn't if I were you, old boy. They pushed our chaps out this morning and retook it. I've just brought my mortars up, so we're having a go at them in a minute or two. I'd get back as soon as possible if I were you.'

Such a nice man!

As I set off back to the airstrip there was a bang – the captain's first mortar was obviously on its way. Or was it? If so, what was that second bang so much nearer? And that fountain of earth sixty yards to the right? The Japs were *behind* us, the other way. Then a third one, nearer and noisier, and another fountain of earth.

It clicked. It wasn't the Captain mortaring the Japs: it was the Japs mortaring *us*, and the causeway, being right on the skyline, made us a perfect target. I took the bomb-chicane at a speed that would have had Michael Schumacher green with envy, and without skidding into one of the craters. Had we done so the Japs would have been able to mortar us at leisure. And I'd left my water bottle behind in the Harvard. Even if the Japs hadn't done us in immediately, I wouldn't have fancied a day being fried alive in the crater by that blazing sun with no water as I waited for night to fall before we could crawl out.

'Shame about that', I lied to my crew when we got back to the airstrip. 'Let me know when we've retaken the bomb dump, and I'll come back.'

As I spoke, the earth beneath my feet trembled, and a few seconds later came the sound of an almighty explosion, and a cloud of smoke rose on the horizon. The Japs had blown their bomb dump to kingdom come, so I readily forgave them for mortaring us.

As I flew happily back to Monywa I realised that the Harvard I was flying was a fully aerobatic machine, so decided to celebrate with a few high jinks. Well, low jinks, really. Pat and I had brought our heavy camp kits with us in case we'd had to stay the night, and they were lying loose in the luggage compartment, so I couldn't do any inverted stuff or negative G. I settled for a loop, but as it was some time since I'd done one I played for safety. I didn't want to stall and fall off the top of the loop as I did in that Anson – only six years ago was it? So I did it at high speed. Warning Pat in the back seat of my intentions, I dived to get up plenty of speed and hauled back on the stick with both hands, pulling all the G in the world. I was mystified to fly into a grey cloud, which rapidly degenerated into solid black. There hadn't been a cloud in the sky when I'd started, so what on earth was going on? I heard the engine gaining revs, so I was probably on the down side of the loop. I slapped the throttle shut, the G forces decreased, the black cloud became grey, and the grey vanished. The sky was as clear as when I'd started. Not a cloud in sight! For the first and only time in my life I'd blacked out!

A few seconds later Pat Ironside's voice came over the intercom from the back cockpit. Scarcely able to conceal the admiration in his voice he asked, 'How on *earth* do you control an aircraft in a situation like that, sir?'

I felt it better for my reputation not to tell him that I hadn't a clue.

I wrote to HQ South-East Asia that, regrettably, the Japs had blown up the bomb dump, so their bright idea would not come to fruition. And sincerely hoped that no more Jap bomb dumps would fall into our hands.

One of the strategies of the Burma campaign was to fight, to a certain extent, in areas where the disease rate was high, which at first sight sounds quite daft, but the Japanese medical services were known to be well below our standard, and we had DDT, a potent germ-killer which we could spray from the air with our Hurricanes and Spitfires. Before we went into an area it was given a good dose of DDT from the air, the most efficient solvent for DDT being a colourless liquid, but we didn't use it as it could so easily be interpreted as germ warfare, so it was dissolved in the stannic chloride which we used for our smoke screens, as when covering an Army attack. (Mind you, I still wish that the disease rate in Burma had been lower, but I suppose that in warfare one has to consider the broad strategic picture, as seen by those higher up the ladder.)

A few weeks after my trip to Meiktila our HQ moved down there, but unfortunately we had run out of DDT, and it soon showed. The battle for the town had been hotly contested, and there were Jap bodies all over the place, including in the lake from which we drew our drinking-water. So I added dysentery to my already fashionable ringworm and scabies. But Dey Ma, the bearer who'd looked after me since I'd recruited him at Indainggye, felt that Meiktila was too far from his home, and asked to leave. I couldn't just jettison him all those miles away from his family, and so, as I had to visit one of my back-area units, I diverted a little and flew him to an abandoned airstrip not too far away from his home. Already, only a few weeks after the Thunderbolt squadrons had left, nature was reclaiming its own – scrub was sprouting through the *kutcha* (beaten earth) surface and growing at the sides. As I helped Dey Ma out of the back cockpit two bullock carts swayed out of a track and crossed the strip, and he was offered a lift. I said goodbye to him, and took off on my official assignment, and from what I'd seen I imagine that within a couple of months that strip would have become almost unidentifiable paddy again.

But there remained water-shortage problems at Meiktila. We were no longer living on the banks of a river where we could take a refreshing swim, and perhaps catch the occasional fish. The water ration was reduced to 1½ gallons a day, less that required by the cookhouse. So after ensuring that my water bottle was full in case I had to dash off somewhere, I washed and shaved in the morning, leaving the soapy, whiskery water in the canvas wash-basin, to be used as a freshener at midday. And if I could stand the sight of it I even hoarded it till eventide in my fairly unproductive attempts to get on top of my ringworm and scabies.

It was during this period that I experienced one of the many sad stories of the war. The majority of supply drops to deep-penetration jitter parties such as the Chindits was done by transport Dakotas, which could carry 6,000 lb of stores into make-do airstrips, but in very jungly country away from the strips our Spitfires and Hurricanes backed them up with small 250 lb parachute containers. Every now and again, if there was room, some well-meaning person would slip in the occasional bottle of whisky as a treat, but there was a feeling that not all of it was getting through. I was not involved in the planning of these operations, but as the containers were carried on my aircraft's bomb-racks I had to see the Army about some detail or other. I flew down and found the organising Captain and Sergeant in their tent at the side of the airstrip. They both looked a bit bleary-eyed, *and smelt of alcohol!* It was daytime, and anyway we only got three bottles of beer a month, so this must be the solution to the vanishing whisky. I chatted them up, and as I did, my initial indignation with them for robbing men doing a dangerous job miles inside Japland was tempered as we discussed the problem I had come to sort out. Neither of them seemed to meet my eye – they seemed to be gazing at something a couple of miles away over my shoulder. And everything was a bit vague. They seemed to exist in an untroubled world of their own. They were, poor souls, as far round the bend as anyone I ever met. Gradually, I got their story. Before the war they had been tea planters in Assam, and in September 1939 they were due for their triennial six months' home leave, but with the outbreak of the war they had immediately joined up. But in the *Indian* Army, in whose eyes Burma was a 'home service' station – a bit like being posted from England to Scotland. Whatever leave they had – and *I* certainly got no leave during my fifteen months out there – would have been short ones back in India. They hadn't seen their wives and children in England for *seven years*, and seemed a bit vague about them anyway.

I didn't split on them.

It looked as though the monsoon was not all that far away, as we had a heavy rainfall one night. It thundered down on the roof of my tent so menacingly that I went out to hammer the tent pegs harder into the ground, but to no avail. We were camped on a slope, and the whole hill slipped ten feet downhill. All my private possessions were submerged in mud, including all the precious letters from home. I just gave up, and lay in my soaking tent, sleeping fitfully till morning, when I could start to wring things out and hang them on trees to dry. Except for all the letters from home which I used to read and reread. They were just pulp.

But things were now easing up, and with nobody, including the Japs, flying at night we had the occasional luxury of a live ENSA show – good old-fashioned music hall stuff that went a good way to raising morale, and then one memorable night when a travelling film unit gave a show. They slung the screen between two trees and we all sat on the ground, except for those who elected for the dress circle, climbing trees and squatting in the branches like a bunch of monkeys. But the choice of film was unfortunate – it featured Errol Flynn commanding a platoon of about twenty men in Burma, and achieving the most phenomenal success through incredible feats of bravery. Catcalls multiplied, people wondering audibly why our boss, General Bill Slim, kept so many of us out there when all he had to do to finish the job was to send for Errol Flynn. As the uproar increased, a particularly agitated bunch of soldiers shook their branch of a tree so violently that it broke off, bringing them rapidly to earth amid initial roars of laughter all round. Fortunately, just one broken leg.

Mandalay fell, and I made a hasty diversion to that romantic place, but couldn't make head or tail of that patriotic song that used to be bellowed out in the music halls – 'On the road to Mandalay/Where the flying-fishes play/And the sun comes up like thunder/Out of China 'cross the bay.' China was a million miles to the north, and the sun rises in the east, for God's sake. I didn't see a single flying-fish either. Maybe I'd got the song wrong.

Then Rangoon was captured, our attack being encouraged by the message written in white paint on the roof of Changi jail by the recently released prisoners of war. 'JAPS GONE', it said for the benefit of reconnaissance aircraft. And we were to move our headquarters there, hopefully before the monsoon broke.

I was called in to the Planning Department – known to most of us as the 'fuck-em-up-brigade' – and detailed to lead the main road party the 150 miles to Rangoon in fifty three-ton trucks and a few Jeeps, all of which I had to sign for personally at the local Army Ordnance depot. 'You should get there in three days at the most, and you'll have a couple of Engineers' trucks to help with breakdowns.'

Having watched all those John Wayne Westerns in childhood I had longed to do such a job, and with my standard flying-kit of revolver, water bottle and machete clanging from my webbing belt as I organised the convoy I felt that I probably looked the part, too – 'Wagons roll', and so on. But an hour before the start the Transport Officer dashed up and said that a couple of fifteen-hundredweight trucks would also be joining the convoy, with something that sounded like wazzbeez.

'What on earth is Wazzbeez?'

'Plural, old boy. Wasbees – Women's Auxiliary Service, Burma.'

'*Women!* We'll be three or four days on the road, and there are Jap jitter parties about.'

If women were coming my John Wayne image lay in ruins. I unbuckled my belt and put it in the back of the Jeep.

'Anyway, what do Wasbees do?'

'Sort of NAAFI canteen, only they're all volunteers – bit like the VADs at home. Dish out tea and sympathy to the troops. Bunch of leathery old colonels' wives, I'm told.'

I told my second-in-command to put the Wasbees in the middle of the convoy, with instructions to the trucks ahead and behind to defend them to the death if need be, and we set off south on rapidly deteriorating roads. In the afternoon one of the three-tonners had to be abandoned with a broken mainspring, and as we were reorganising its load onto other trucks one of the leathery old colonels' wives approached. Only she wasn't *very* leathery. In fact she was a 19-year-old Australian stunner of a blonde with a husky voice, an English rose complexion, and a mug of tea in her hand. Her name was Colin, though she looked *very* feminine.

'I've put two lumps of sugar in it', she said.

How did she know?

Those girls worked hard. They and their equipment had rattled and banged in the back of their trucks over God-awful roads for hours on end, yet within twenty minutes of halting they'd got their pump-up Primus stoves going and produced gallons of tea for the whole convoy.

We laagered for the night near a battery of 25-pounders, and I put the Wasbees in the centre of a square of trucks for security. Half-way through the night there was an unholy crash, and shells went howling over our heads. The crashes and howls continued as we sprang awake to repel the jitter party. The only people in the RAF who knew anything about ground fighting were the RAF Regiment, but we hadn't got any, and anyway it was night-time. We *were* armed, of course, every man having his rifle, Sten gun or revolver, and every man was determined to sell his life dearly against the invading horde. As the Duke of Wellington said of his men before Waterloo, 'I don't know if they frighten the enemy, but by God they frighten *me*.' The Duke had an easy ride compared with what I had on my hands. In the darkness men with loaded guns, some on full automatic, bumped into one another. The 25-pounders continued their mind-numbing crashes. The shells howled overhead. Occasional shots, accidental in my opinion, rang out. I grabbed a torch from a passing member of the *dementia* and swept it round the perimeter without seeing a single one of the Duke of Edinburgh's slitty-eyed faces, and found the Wasbees, understandably apprehensive, crouched on the ground beneath the tarpaulin they'd slung between some trees. 'Is it a jitter party?' asked the boss. I tried to jolly her out of it. 'Worse, I'm afraid. It's the RAF. But you'd better lie low until it's all over.'

The 25-pounders eventually stopped, as, fortunately, did my own men, so I went across to talk to the battery commander.

'What was all that about?'

'There's a crossroads in Japland a mile and a half over there, so we let them have a few rounds at irregular intervals to keep them on their toes. Wakes them up a bit, you know.'

'Woke *us* up, too, old boy.'

When we drove into the Ordnance depot in Rangoon a couple of days later, they took my word for the vehicles we'd had to abandon on the road, and happily I seemed to have one more Jeep in the convoy than there was on their manifest. Thinking rapidly on my feet, I explained that that one was RAF property, and drove off in what was to become my personal transport for the rest of my stay in Rangoon.

With several others, I was quartered in an abandoned house, and on the first night was intrigued to hear what sounded like a cattle market nearby. Taking a torch to track down the noise, I solved the problem. Most houses had 'tanks' – rectangular excavations in the garden filled with water, in case of drought or fire – and at the edge of one sat an enormous bullfrog, the water below being dotted with the heads of a dozen or more of what I presumed were adoring cowfrogs. The boss frog inflated his huge throat sac and let go a fantastically loud and long bellow, the massed sycophants in the water below replying at a similar volume. It wasn't quite Handel's *Water Music*, but to the background of multiple 'BOOM-BOOMs' I drifted off to sleep.

Another aquatic feature of Burmese life was the water buffaloes, who cooled off after their day's work by lying up to their necks in water, and I was amused to see a dog doing the same in a draining ditch at the side of the road. He had a slightly bemused expression on his face, as though he knew that there was good thinking behind whatever he was doing, but wasn't quite sure what.

Having achieved our aim of getting to Rangoon before the monsoon broke, some of us now realised that we were perhaps a little bit tired. Then VE-Day came, and enthusiastic letters from home poured in. It *was* wonderful, of course, *really* wonderful, but it was rather a long way away.

But maybe, at last, they'd now send us some better equipment, not the rejects of the war in Europe – ammunition that didn't jam our 20 mm guns, for instance, and locking blocks for those guns that would be guaranteed to hold the breech closed, not the dodgy ones with fractures that *our* pilots had to use. If one of those blocks gave way the released pressure could blow the wing off a Spitfire or Hurricane.

I was not alone in greeting the colossal achievement in Europe in this slightly grudging way: the malaise was fairly prevalent, and our Supremo, Admiral Lord Louis Mountbatten, flew in from Ceylon to give us a pep talk. He gave the overall assessment of the campaign as it had progressed so far, praised our part in it, then went on to give us the projection for the future. It was expected to take another eighteen months to push the Japs up through Indo-China and into China, from where a joint British/Chinese force would invade Japan from the west, and the Americans from the Pacific. Casualties were estimated at 300,000.

'But we can do it', said Louis.

His impact was formidable. And such was his charisma that

by the time he'd finished we *knew* that we could rouse ourselves from our lethargy and do the job. To our cheers, he stepped down from the soap box that had so conveniently been discovered for him, and we dismissed, well fired up.

But that night, scratching away at my scabies and ringworm in the sweating humidity, reality returned. *Eighteen* more months! Three hundred *thousand* more casualties! Tudor and Teddy both dead at the age of 26 and *my* 26th due in a few months. And both our mothers widowed. Guy could be four and the yet-to-be Susan two years or more if I survived to see them again. And not a sight of Christine, of course. I appreciate that I was a staff wallah, but things *do* happen, even in stooge jobs. Think of the Royal Engineers' persecution of me out here – setting off tons of bombs under my nose, and having a go at shattering my propeller. And the Japs trying it on with their mortars. And I was fed up with my face, too, yellow-hued by the anti-malaria tablets we all took.

I didn't *want* another eighteen months away from home.

Then I was posted back to India, going by sea to Calcutta, with a single cabin. Months of tented living must have blunted my senses somewhat, as at first it seemed unimaginable luxury – running water, flushing loo, clean sheets and so on. But by the end of the day I noticed that the ancient washing bowl had black-stained cracks, as had the loo, and that the paintwork was chipped to hell. But it *was* luxury, with gin and tonic before lunch. I had no complaints.

I was posted to a comparable staff post near Delhi, but it was a nuts-and-bolts job in a Maintenance Group servicing all the aircraft in the Far East, and I was dreadfully miscast. Bouncing bombs on Hurricanes and hang-ups on Spitfires I could get my teeth into, but the Progress Report on Modification 254/1945 to Gun Turret Rotating Service Joints left me cold. However, there was a big bonus – my units were scattered the length and breadth of India. From romantic Peshawar in the North-West Frontier, where Afridi tribesmen openly strode the streets with rifles slung from their shoulders, to Trichinopoly in the south; from Karachi in the west to Calcutta in the east, I flew the length and breadth of India, staying in Maharajas' palaces and bamboo messes where bandicoots wandered in and out. I saw the Taj Mahal from the air fifty years before Princess Diana sat so sadly in front of it. And my log-book tells me that for every two days I spent in the office I spent one in the air – really good for a staff wallah. That aspect of the job was a broadening and relaxing experience, as I never got any leave during my time in the East.

On one station I was packing my suitcase to fly on to the next destination when an enormous bullfrog hopped into the room. I wasn't into frogs, so tried to chase him out, but he was having none of it. He got into a corner and started leaping higher and higher, so in case he leapt up my trousers I set about doing other things, and by the time I'd completed my preparations for leaving he had vanished. On a three-day trip I had to carry a fair amount of clothes and paperwork, and I had to force down the lid of my over-stuffed suitcase by sitting on it. When I opened it at my next destination I was mystified to see what appeared to be a lady's crocodile-skin handbag lying on top of my clothes. Only it wasn't a handbag; it was the unfortunate frog, who'd hopped in when my back was turned. Squashed flat and burst open, he had made a real mess of the clothes.

But my biggest bonus was on the way home via Karachi, where I spotted a *five*-bladed propeller among the aircraft parked on the tarmac. I ran the Flight Commander to earth, but he was adamant. 'Sorry, old boy, it's the Station Commander's personal runabout – a Mark Umpteen Spitfire. He'd have my guts for garters if I lent it to you.'

But he was a kindly soul. 'Look, would a Mustang do instead?'

Would it not! It would bring my total of types flown to three dozen, and I got out quickly before he changed his mind. It was the hottest machine I ever flew, and one thing that impressed me was that you could select just which pair of 50-calibre Brownings you wished to fire – all six for blasting things at close range, or just two or four if you thought there was a long slog ahead. I took it up to altitude and got 500 mph out of her. Then it struck me that after six years of war an elderly 28-year-old with a wife and two children back home, with both our mothers widowed and with my two brothers killed, I'd better not push things too far. I cut the throttle and landed.

Awaiting me when I got back to Delhi was a letter offering me a Medium Service Commission, which I declined. A Permanent Commission, yes, but if I *had* to leave the RAF I would get out at the age of 28, with more hope of finding a job.

Then they dropped those wonderful atom bombs, and we were all to go home. Demobilisation was the only topic of conversation, and criticism of the demob system grew as it was realised that the men in Europe were getting a better deal than we were, as it was going to take a hell of a lot of shipping, and a month at sea, to get us all home. There were protest 'strikes' at some of the units in India, only they weren't strikes, of course, they were mutinies. Fortunately, there were none at any of *my* units, because just how I would have coped with a mutiny I had no idea. After nine years in the service my instinctive reaction would have been to clamp down hard on the mutineers. But after six years of war and millions of dead I was heartily fed up with things, and I didn't want to end my career being lynched by a crowd of angry airmen after I'd shot a couple of them to maintain discipline.

At last my demob number came up, and I was to go home. I *would* miss the flying, but I wasn't going to do myself harm in a final aerobatic fling, as a chap called Cobber Cain had done in France in 1940. Before going back to England to collect his DFC from the King he did one last celebratory beat-up of his airfield, came in too low and killed himself when he hit the deck. I intended to go home in one piece, so shut my log-book.

At the embarkation unit in Bombay I appealed for help to get rid of my ringworm and scabies: I didn't want go home in my present lousy state.

'Don't worry about it', said the Medical Officer. 'The voyage home will take a month, so it will improve a lot. And anyway, it will be so cold in England that a couple of days there will kill the bugs off.'

'But I don't want to pass them on to my family.'

'Highly improbable.'

'But I *might*.'

'Oh, all right, if you insist. Try this ointment. Next!'

I felt that he, too, had been a long time overseas, and had lost interest. As had the dentist who, after a short look into my mouth, yanked out three precious molar teeth.

I was given a draft of 2,500 men to bring home, their administration keeping me well occupied on the long voyage, and fortunately for my peace of mind – and probably because they too were going home at long last – they all behaved pretty well: I didn't have to shoot a single one.

We docked at Liverpool early on the morning of Christmas Eve 1945, and entrained for a demobilisation centre in Staffordshire, where they had run out of coal the day before. But they pulled out all the stops to get us home for Christmas, and in the freezing cold that I hoped was giving the scabies mites hell we Far Eastern veterans went through the demob. I signed indemnities admitting liability for all RAF equipment which while under my care might have been culpably lost, stolen or strayed, thankful that they hadn't tossed in the cost of those three crashed aircraft. They gave me a ration book and clothing cards, and told me where to collect my demob outfit of civilian clothes. In a vast refrigerated aircraft hangar, which differed somewhat from Gieves' hallowed premises in Bond Street, 2,500 assorted ranks were selecting the civilian clothes which they were to receive from a grateful country. With Civvie Street just round the corner, six years of deference were swept aside, and it was a case of the survival of the fittest. Holding up a garment that looked slightly less awful than many, I was affronted to have it snatched out of my hands by an AC2. Spivs, foreseeing the clothing shortage, were active, perhaps briefed by their families at home. They roamed the place with wads of notes and bulging bin bags.

'Wanna sell those?' asked a shifty-eyed individual of me. 'I'll give you three pounds for the jacket and four for the overcoat – seven pounds ten for the two.' I took a second look at the things I was holding. If the spiv thought they were good enough to buy they must be better than I had imagined. I drew myself to my full height.

'I'm sorry. I have no wish to part with them', and marched off with a jacket that proved to be a little bit tight under the armpits, and an unpleasantly coloured overcoat whose hem sagged two inches on one side after the first rainstorm. On account of its colour Christine would call it my 'dog-dirt coat'.

I crammed my acquisitions into the bag provided, and along with thirty others boarded the three-tonner which was to take me away from the only life I'd known for the last 9½ years, and down to the station, where I gave in my travel voucher for the journey home, where they handed me a *third*-class ticket.

Already a bit depressed at having to quit the service, I felt that it was a scurvy trick to play. For all those years they'd carted me round in first class, but now that I wasn't necessary they had sent me on my way in the cheapest possible manner. But the depression soon lifted – maybe the ticket had just been a mistake by an Orderly Room clerk. We drew in to the station, and as I got off the train, clutching my suitcase and bag of clothing, I felt sure that the crusaders of old had returned from their wars in much more style than I, but who cared! In a few minutes' time I'd meet up with Christine and Guy again for the first time in over a year. And meet Susan for the first time. And what could beat that as a Christmas present?

While I was overseas Christine had been given the use of her mother's planned retirement home, a little house a hundred yards from the beach in the Lancashire village of Knott End-on-Sea, facing the fishing port of Fleetwood on the other bank of the River Wyre. At low tide the children caught crabs and other creatures marooned in the shallow pools. And perhaps twice a week, the chip shop, with its good connections with Fleetwood, displayed the 'Frying Tonight' sign, so welcome in those days when, with the slow-down in American aid, rationing was even more severe than it had been during the war. For two shillings – 10p – we got fish and chips for the four of us. And the chip shop was also a much-valued gossip exchange.

I'd had no leave while I was overseas, and with my demobilisation allowance it added up to two months on full pay, so there was no great hurry to find a job. Christine's mother came to look after the children and we took off for a week in London, during which I discovered a new Christine. Having had to fend for herself for so long she was very capable, my first introduction to the new woman being when we booked into the Strand Palace Hotel. As I put down our suitcase to get the swing door in motion she strode ahead like an Amazon and gave it such a push that it was up to maximum revs in no time. I followed obediently, and through all the other doors which she shoved open. We had a very enjoyable seven days of sophistication – a very pleasant introduction to my new life. But home again, when she was bathing the children, she pointed to a mark on Susan's tummy.

'What on earth's that?'

'Ringworm', I said with authority.

'Ringworm? How on earth could she get ringworm?'

'From me, I suppose.'

'You've got *ringworm* and haven't told me?'

'Sorry! I forgot about it in the excitement of getting home. Thought I'd been cured by the cold weather. We'll have to take her to the doctor first thing in the morning.'

'But what on earth will Andrew think of us with a disease like that in the family?'

Andrew had a thing about her, and this might knock her off her pedestal.

Slinking into the surgery next morning, she said she thought Susan had ringworm.

'Nonsense, Mrs Edwards. Ringworm is a disease of neglect and dirt, the sort of thing you find in inner-city slums. Whatever it is, I can assure you that it won't be ringworm.'

The nappy was removed.

'Oh dear!'

He wrote a prescription and Christine returned, not in the best of moods.

'Andrew said that ringworm was a disease of neglect and dirt. I felt *awful*.'

She rabbited on at length.

'Well, we *were* a bit grubby at times – short of water and so on. Used it for drinking mostly.'

Might as well get it all over in one. 'I picked up scabies as well', I tossed in.

'Scabies? What on earth's that?'

'Sort of itching of the skin.'

No way could I tell her about the livestock angle.

The pharmacy being next to the chip shop gossip exchange, we kept things to ourselves by crossing the ferry to Fleetwood to buy Susan's ringworm ointment.

Then Christine developed scabies. I'd been watching the symptoms develop with some trepidation – a hand wandering to rub a certain area; its return to scratch gently a few minutes later; then with increasing vigour. When the penny dropped, a virago surfaced, and it was some time before a constructive discussion could take place. And if I'd let on that there were *live* mites burrowing within her skin she really *would* have blown her top.

'I'm not going back to Andrew with yet another skin disease in the family, and that's final', she stated.

'We don't have to: I saw an advert about a skin disease ointment in the paper. I'll send off for some.'

The *Dermodeath*, when it arrived, was obviously a high-quality product, the packet being covered with glowing recommendations from an obviously well-connected clientele – in the accompanying illustrations a few of them seemed to be wearing ermine and coronets. *Dermodeath* was obviously a nationally acclaimed success against the most hideous diseases known to man.

The instructions were simple – run a hot bath, stir in the recommended amount of powder, and soak yourself for twenty minutes.

'I'll double the dose, just to make sure', said Christine.

'It *does* say, 'Do not exceed the stated dose.''

I was over-ridden, but while the double dose didn't cure our scabies it *did*, to Christine's fury, remove all the glazing off the bath below the waterline.

Then I had an idea. 'I'm on demob leave, still officially in the Air Force, so I'll get into uniform and nip over to see the Medical Officer at Westbrook: he might have some ideas.'

The MO pronounced the ringworm cured, and said he'd fix the scabies. 'This benzoyl bisulphate will kill the little buggers off in no time. Take a hot bath to open up the pores, and cover yourselves from head to foot in it. You'll be cured by the weekend.'

When we'd got the children to bed I soaked in the bath, dried off, and rubbed in the cool, soothing lotion. For the first time in months I felt really clean.

As I lay reading on the bed Christine repeated the process, then lay alongside me, by which time a pleasant warmth had spread over my skin. Well, more *heat* than warmth when you came to think about it. Yes, *heat*. That was the correct word. And getting hotter by the minute. Without warning, I went incandescent from head to foot, and shot bellowing off the bed.

'What on earth's the matter?' asked Christine.

'You're about to find out.'

'For heaven's sake keep your voice down, you'll wake the children.'

But the look of irritation on her face was replaced by apprehension, and when the incandescent phase set in no Venus rose from the waves quicker than she. Her skin had turned scarlet and her language blue. But eventually we both came off the boil and flopped onto the bed, exhausted by a traditional service cure: as the scabies mites lived in the surface half-millimetre of the skin, the Benzoyl Bisulphate burned off the top millimetre, just to make sure. We were cured, and on speaking terms again.

I started job hunting, answering about thirty advertisements without a single acknowledgement. Day after day after depressing day, footsteps passed in the street outside as those lucky people in work made their way to bus stop or ferry slip.

Then a ray of light pierced the gloom. Ambrose, a family friend living in London, was a celebrated BBC music critic, millions listening to his deep, resonant voice on the radio, and reading his crits in the papers. He would put me up for the night and arrange an appointment at Broadcasting House for me to be tested as a potential announcer, and he had two tickets for the opera which he was to review the night before my interview. Before we set off for Covent Garden Ambrose poured a couple of stiff whiskies apiece, and to recover from the stress of the tube journey called in at the Opera House bar for another. After blundering our belated way into the stalls he immediately fell into a deep sleep, waking only when the prima donna let go a real earful of decibels.

'This woman's got a voice like a chainsaw ripping up live donkeys. Let's go to the bar.'

During the interval admirers swarmed round Ambrose, lapping up his opinions as fast as we lapped up the whiskies which were being thrust upon him, and upon me as his protégé. Women swooned round him, listening to not a word he said, just drinking in those mellifluous tones.

When the audience returned to their seats we stayed behind to work our way through the backlog of whiskies lined up on the bar, and I grew uneasy on Ambrose's behalf.

'Ambrose, what about your crit for *The Clarion*? Hadn't we better get back and listen to the opera?'

'Half a mo'.' He rummaged through his pockets and produced a sheaf of papers. 'Ah, yes. Here it is. All safe and sound.'

'You've already written it!'

'Yeees. I've known this company for years, so know exactly how they'll deliver. And if anything untoward happens I've got a pal backstage who'll tip me the wink. F'rinstance, if that old cow drops dead in the third act a contact in BBC archives will let me have her obituary. I'll update it with tonight's outstanding performance and collect a packet syndicating it to the morning papers.'

So that was how things worked!

The Fat Lady was still at it when we finished the booze and staggered back to the flat. And about ten minutes later – or so it seemed – a bag-eyed Ambrose shook me awake. At Broadcasting House, with aching head, I talked into a microphone. They played it back, suggesting improvements. I announced the Fat Stock Prices to the studio wall: 'Fat cattle per live hundredweight', followed by the shipping forecast: 'Dogger, Fisher, German Bight', I told the unlistening trawlermen.

They were all very kind, and gave me every chance, but they

wanted the Ambrose touch, and I hadn't got it.

The weeks dragged by. Our savings, so carefully hoarded during our Burma days, dwindled rapidly. Out of the next batch of letters I wrote in answer to various advertisements I received only three replies, all in the negative. Even my application for a job of assistant jobbing gardener was turned down, though I *did* get an interview for a white-collar job of sorts. It rained when I went for it, and the right hem of my 'dog-dirt' demob overcoat sagged even lower than usual. I suppose I didn't really look the part, and didn't get it. And when one of the staff commiserated with me I asked his opinion as to whether the demob overcoat might have contributed to my failure.

'I don't think so, but they *can* be pretty awful, can't they? My wife gave mine to the dog for his basket.'

There was a respite when a trawler ran aground on the sands, and along with other members of the leisured classes we walked the half-mile across the sands to where she lay on her side.

'I suppose she'll float off with the next tide', I said to a gaffer in the crowd.

'Not a hope: she's neaped. By the time there's enough water to float her off her back will be broken.'

Which it was.

'She's a write-off now, of course', I said to another gaffer on our second trip out.

'Not until the Receiver of Wreck says so, she ain't.'

'Where does he hang out?'

'In Preston. Daft, ain't it? Miles from the sea!'

Far enough to be safe for a while, I felt. I ran a predatory eye over her and decided that the most saleable portable items were the pulley blocks. I took a sack and a kit of tools and went back to where she had now settled into four feet of water at an angle of thirty degrees, Stripping to my underpants – I was half a mile from the shoreline – I waded across and boarded. After a couple of hours struggling with rusty bolts on the sloping deck I'd flung a dozen or so of the heavy blocks onto the dry sand near my clothes, but the canted mast was more difficult. The only way to get at those blocks was to crook my legs over the cross trees and hang upside down. Using one hand to hold on for safety meant that I could only work with one, which was difficult and undignified, but the time must have passed quickly as I heard the sound of voices, and saw Christine and the children coming across the sands. Unfortunately, they were accompanied by a Pillar of the Church, who was also a magistrate! His expression highly critical, he gazed up at me hanging upside down from my perch like a naked ape, my still-wet underpants leaving little to the imagination.

'Good morning, Mr Shufflebotham,' I bleated, 'lovely day to be out.'

It was an unfortunate choice of words. In Mr Shufflebotham's circle 'out' meant 'out of prison'. And could a charge of indecent exposure be laid, leading to a custodial sentence? I wished he would go away, so flung the next pulley block to fall as near to him as possible. He took the hint and left, not to alert the Receiver of Wreck, I hoped. I shinned to the top of the mast, freed the masthead light, and waded ashore to join the family.

But the loot weighed about a hundredweight, and I was half a mile from home. Sending the family ahead with the tools and masthead light, and telling them to keep a good lookout for police and things, I dragged the load home. I lay low for a couple of days, but nothing approaching what could be a Receiver of Wreck showed up, so I split the load into two sacks that slung more easily over the shoulder and staggered across on the ferry to Fleetwood.

Stopping to regain my breath, I entered the first ship's chandler.

'I've got some pulley blocks for sale', I said brightly. 'Single and double-sheaved. Don't need them any more.'

'Sorry, mate. I can't handle second-hand running gear. Board of Trade regulations.'

'Board of Trade! Who on earth gives a toss about *them*?'

'I do, mate. Can you imagine what would happen if they gave way in a Force 9 gale? Then where would I be?'

'Give way! They're as good as new.'

'Maybe, but I'm not interested.'

I staggered out like a coolie, recovered my breath, and went into the next chandler's.

'I'm laying up my cabin cruiser', I opened. 'So these blocks are going cheap for a quick sale.'

'No way, mate. Can you imagine those ...'

'Giving way in a Force 9?' I finished for him. 'They'd hold the Queen Mary, that lot.'

'Maybe they would, but I can't handle them.'

And neither would any of the others.

I went out and sat miserably on a bollard. They were *very* heavy, but I couldn't just tip them into the dock or I'd be seen.

'Bad luck, mate', I heard a voice behind me. It was another customer who had followed me out.

'If I was you I'd try Long John Silver. He's a bit of a nut case, mind you; lost a leg in a car accident and hasn't been the same since he saw Robert Newton in *Treasure Island*. He's your best bet.'

I took the usual rest, then fought my way into the gloom of the chandlery over piles of chains and cables. As I tripped over yet another obstacle a voice roared out of the darkness 'What's that ye have there, me hearty?'

I suppose he'll have a bloody parrot on his shoulder when he appears, I thought. He hadn't, but the figure limping out of the darkness didn't waste much time.

'What's that then, eh?'

'Some pulley blocks surplus to requirements', I said as I tipped them out on the floor

'How much, boy, how much?'

'Ten pounds.'

'*Ten* quid! Pull the other one. Four at the most.'

Four! That wasn't going to go very far.

'Eight. I couldn't take less.'

'Let's split the difference, boy. I'll go to six.'

I made a final effort. 'Make it guineas and it's a deal. Six *guineas*.'

We shook hands on the deal. And I rather liked the guineas touch – it gave a bit of class to the operation. I bought a box of chocolates for Christine, some Fleetwood rock for the children and slipped into the *Admiral Lord Nelson* for a half of bitter, with still enough left over for a fortnight's housekeeping. It was my first stroke of luck for weeks.

But still nothing seemed to be turning up.

'I think I'll have to rejoin the RAF', I told Christine. 'That is, if you can stand the life of continuous posting from job to job. And if that offer of a Medium Service Commission is still open, of course.'

'Let's see', said the Wing Commander at the Air Ministry as he spun through my records, 'You're a squadron leader with 2,000 hours as a pilot, and you're an armament specialist.' (I shuddered at that, as armament specialists were usually one rank below the general-duties pilots of similar seniority.)

'Er, I'd rather be general duties if possible, sir.'

'Let's see, then. I've got a list of possible vacancies here.'

He ran his pencil down a column and stopped.

'You're illegible for this one.'

Illegible? Where had this guy been to school?

But his voice was monotonous, devoid of inflection. A cheerfully spoken *illegible* might be interpreted as *eligible*, that on a descending note as *ineligible*. How on earth could I get round this chap who made a Year 3 Comprehensive pupil sound like a Harvard professor? I writhed as he continued to go through my file, turning page after page.

Then he dropped a bombshell.

'Oh dear! I missed this. You're short sighted, and possibly night-blind.'

'That's no problem, sir, I fly with corrective lenses.'

'I'm truly sorry, Edwards, but they've changed the regulations recently – all these jet aircraft and things. I'm *really* sorry, but I'm afraid we can't re-employ you.'

And only two more weeks' of overseas pay to come in. He threw me a life-line.

'You'd be very well qualified for the Weapons Branch of the Control Commission for Germany, you know. Why not try that?'

I thought about it on the way home. I *could* try the Control Commission, but that would mean more separation from the family, and I'd had enough of that during the war years. And anyway, it would only be a temporary job until Germany was sorted out. I wanted to settle down.

Maybe I should try the Labour Exchange? In fact I would *have* to try it. There was nothing else.

I took the ferry across to Fleetwood, turned up the collar of my coat to minimise the chance of recognition, and slunk in.

'Can I see your card', asked the clerk behind the counter.

This was more like it. Formal, just like old times. I produced it.

'No, your *card*.'

'That's it – Squadron Leader G. Edwards, RAF.'

'No. Your *stamp* card.'

Only then did I recall that day six years before, when a considerate Air Ministry had advised Regular personnel to contribute to a thing called the National Insurance Scheme. Had it arrived a few months earlier it would have seemed a good investment, but it came at a time in the Norwegian Campaign when already 35% of my original squadron had got the chop, with obviously more to come. The odds against surviving were low, and it seemed a dreadful waste of five shillings (25p) a week. I had screwed up the paper and thrown it in the bin.

'I'm afraid I haven't got *that* sort of card.'

'In that case,' said the clerk in kindly tones, 'I'm afraid you're not eligible for unemployment relief.'

What! Not even the dole … ?

What on earth lay ahead?

And how was I going to explain to Christine?

Since our marriage five years earlier we'd consciously lived a reasonably economical life, saving up for the future, and being greatly helped by the fact that there was little in Burma that I could spend money on in my time out there. We were very chuffed indeed with the £800 we'd got in the bank.

But during the five bitter months which I had to spend on the scrap heap before I landed a job that £800 went walloping down.

I'd been brought down to earth in no uncertain fashion, and even worse, I was taking Christine and the children with me.

But fortunately, better times did lie ahead, even if they were an unconscionable time a-coming.

Index